THE PROSECUTION OF
PROFESSOR CHANDLER DAVIS

In Memoriam: Horace Chandler Davis (1926–2022).

The Prosecution of Chandler Davis

McCarthyism, Communism, and the Myth of Academic Freedom

by STEVE BATTERSON

MONTHLY REVIEW PRESS

New York

Library of Congress Cataloging-in-Publication data
available from the publisher.

ISBN paper: 978-1-68590-035-9
ISBN cloth: 978-1-68590-036-6

Typeset in Bulmer MT

MONTHLY REVIEW PRESS, NEW YORK
monthlyreview.org

5 4 3 2 1

Contents

Foreword

By Ellen Schrecker

The American left has few heroes. We specialize in martyrs like Joe Hill, Albert Parsons, and Malcolm X, and masses like the thousands of young women in the 1909 Shirtwaist strike and the Black teenagers who defied the German Shepherds of Birmingham, Alabama, in 1963. But we also need to be reminded of those individual heroes who, like Chandler Davis, thrust themselves into history because of their intense commitment to a better world. In this all-too-timely exploration of Davis's encounter with McCarthyism during the late 1950s and early 1960s, Steve Batterson shows us how one principled radical managed to stand up against the Cold War witchhunt. Today, as we confront an equally, if not more serious, threat to political dissent and free expression, perhaps Davis's story can inspire similar resistance to the right's current attack on our democratic polity.

A radical activist both before and after he was hired to teach mathematics at the University of Michigan in the early 1950s, Chan, as he was called by those who knew him, had been expecting a summons from the witchhunters. When he received his subpoena from the House Un-American Activities Committee (HUAC) late in 1953, he already knew that he would not tell its members about his political beliefs and activities. But instead of invoking the Fifth Amendment as so many "unfriendly" witnesses, including his own father the year before, had done in order to avoid prosecution for contempt of Congress, Chan decided to rely on the First Amendment's protection of free speech and association. He knew that tactic would be a long shot, but he hoped to pressure the Supreme Court to reverse its earlier acquiescence in the Cold War's Red Scare. As expected, he was not only convicted, serving a six-month sentence in the Danbury Federal Penitentiary, but he was also fired by the University of Michigan and blacklisted by the nearly 150 U.S. mathematics departments to which he applied for a job.

For Chan, his legal battle and struggle against the blacklist was part of a lifelong crusade against political repression. Born to a family of rebels that included ancestors on both sides of the Revolutionary War, a family home that was a stop on the Underground Railroad, a great-grandfather who served as a bodyguard to the abolitionist Wendell Phillips and became a war hero after he was wounded at Antietam, and parents who drifted in and out of the Communist Party (CP) during and after the 1930s, Chan's political activities began in his teens and continued throughout the rest of his life. He joined the CP but did not follow those policies he disagreed with and quietly dropped out a year before his HUAC hearing.

Although punished for his politics, Chan never disavowed his earlier activities or saw himself as a victim. Instead, he viewed his confrontation with HUAC and the following inquisition at the University of Michigan as an opportunity. He willingly risked both his freedom and his career to expose and perhaps even put an end to the mainstream establishment's willingness to quash left-wing political dissent. That his attempt to convince the Supreme Court to reverse its failure to protect the First Amendment almost succeeded is just one of the surprises that

Sup. Ct. → Free speech!

this book reveals. Based on his prodigious research in institutional archives, FBI files, and interviews, Batterson speculates that had Chief Justice Earl Warren not acquiesced in his colleague Felix Frankfurter's refusal to accept a reference to the First Amendment in the draft of an earlier decision about HUAC, Davis might well have won his case.

Instead, in the Supreme Court's June 1959 5–4 decision in the case of the former Vassar instructor Lloyd Barenblatt that was to govern Chan's appeal, Justice John Marshall Harlan based the majority's opinion on a demonized stereotype of American Communism as a Soviet-led conspiracy to destroy the United States government. For that reason, Harlan explained, the Court "has upheld federal legislation aimed at the Communist problem which *in a different context would certainly have raised constitutional issues of the gravest character*" (italics added).[1] In short, the Court's conservative majority assumed, in a flagrant denial of reality, that the small and battered Communist Party posed such a threat to American security that it overrode the Founding Fathers' commitment to free speech.

Batterson's detailed discussion of Davis's simultaneous challenge to the University of Michigan's administrators and faculty leaders who recommended his dismissal offers further evidence of how thoroughly even such a liberal institution as the university collaborated with McCarthyism. Davis refused to answer questions about his political beliefs at the Michigan investigation because they were identical with the ones HUAC had asked him. Were he to do so, it would be "abandoning the principle I defended" at his congressional hearing. "My reason for refusing to answer is . . . based on my desire to defend free speech against what I believe are encroachments by the Committee. . . . I objected to the Committee's questions. The basis of this objection is expressed in the First Amendment."

Chan hoped to persuade the faculty committees considering his dismissal that they should ignore the commonly held stereotypes about Communists and instead judge him by his behavior

at the university and by what his thoroughly supportive departmental colleagues said about his character and activities. Further
bolstering Davis's case was the testimony of Clement Markert
and Mark Nickerson, the two other Michigan professors who
had taken the Fifth Amendment at the same HUAC hearing but
agreed to discuss their politics with the university's panel. But so
toxic was the whiff of Communism that, despite the faculty committees' support for them, the administration fired Nickerson and
planned to let Markert go. Chan's refusal to answer the questions
of the university's interrogators allowed his faculty interlocutors,
who knew he threatened nothing except bigotry and ignorance,
to invoke the commonly held assumptions about the devious
behavior of Communists and claim that since he refused to *prove*
he was not in the Party, his insistence on principle may well have
been insincere. So, out he had to go. It took nearly fifty years for
the university to apologize.

Although Batterson's narrative ends when Chan's confrontation with the Red Scare does and he, his wife, the eminent
historian Natalie Zemon Davis, and children moved to Canada,
his commitment to equality, peace, and freedom never wavered.
His main regret during the 1950s, as he battled the House committee, the university, and the courts, was that having to focus on
his own case kept him from participating in the other progressive causes of that time. Once out of prison and ensconced in a
secure academic position, he resumed that political work, struggling against nuclear weapons, racism, sexism, the Vietnam War,
and the repression of dissent in the United States and elsewhere,
including within the Soviet Union.

With courage, intelligence, and more than a little wit, Chan's
principled commitment to human rights during a grim period of
political repression is genuinely inspirational. At a moment when
the powers-that-be were caving in to reactionary witchhunters,
Chandler Davis stood firm. It mattered then—and it matters
now. Nearly seventy years later, as we confront a reactionary
campaign of censorship and misinformation directed against

teaching the truth about the racism, sexism, and other forms of oppression that have blighted our nation's history, Chan's principled opposition to McCarthyism should encourage us to speak truth to power in the hope that we have learned enough from the past to ensure that his all-too-lonely brand of political heroism will no longer be required.

why this one guy?

Preface

In 2010, fellow mathematician Chandler Davis and I were among a group participating in a hike during a workshop at the Banff International Research Center. I was familiar with Chandler's 1950s ordeal with the House Un-American Activities Committee. He was subpoenaed to testify before a Subcommittee investigating Communist activities in the state of Michigan. In these hearings people with Communist backgrounds, such as Chandler, were asked to admit to their alleged subversive activity and to reveal the names of their associates. The only course for avoiding implication of others, without exposing oneself to prosecution for contempt, was to refuse to answer political questions on the basis of the Fifth Amendment. The downside of relying on the Constitutional right against self-incrimination was exposure to public scorn and likely blacklisting from employment. Chandler took the unusual stance of declining to cooperate with the Subcommittee on the basis of the First Amendment. Subsequently, he was fired from an instructorship at the University of Michigan, convicted for contempt of Congress, and served a six-month sentence in a federal penitentiary.

Curious to learn more details of Chandler's experience but uncertain of the sensitivities, I inquired whether it would be okay for me to ask some questions about his case, mentioning that I would understand if the topic was too uncomfortable for him. Chandler's response was something to the effect: "Why should I be uncomfortable? I did nothing wrong." I only wish I had recorded our conversation as we trudged up and down the mountain.

My understanding of Chandler's story was from a chapter of Ellen Schrecker's excellent book, *No Ivory Tower*, about the treatment of Communist faculty on American college campuses during the McCarthy era.[1] While the legacy of Joseph McCarthy persists as a disgraceful episode in the history of the United States, some of its manifestations are largely forgotten. Indeed, when I broach the topic of the Chandler Davis case with other mathematicians, rarely do they express any familiarity with it.

On the hike, Chandler graciously answered my questions. There was much to his story. If I had not recently begun to research a book on another topic, my enthusiasm from our discussion might have prompted me to take up this project in 2010. Six years later, I completed the other book and shifted my attention to Chandler.

I was fascinated by the First Amendment aspects of the case. Why had Chandler taken an avenue that had already failed for screenwriter Dalton Trumbo and the Hollywood Ten who did their time in 1950? Why did others following the same course, such as folksinger Pete Seeger, go free? It would take time for me to understand these issues.

All along I was struck by Chandler's testimony and the minority opinion of Supreme Court Justice Hugo Black in the 5–4 *Barenblatt*[2] decision that sent Chandler to prison. These powerful statements were available on the internet, if one sought them out. Other relevant materials were more remote.

Ellen Schrecker discovered records from the University of

Michigan investigation, which resulted in Chandler's firing, in the Bentley Historical Library in Ann Arbor. These materials were available to researchers making a trip to Michigan. Since the publication of Schrecker's book, the papers of the House Un-American Activities Committee have been opened for inspection at the National Archives in Washington, DC. A Freedom of Information Act request brought me Chandler's FBI files, after two and a half years of waiting in a National Archives queue. Papers of former Supreme Court justices, at the Library of Congress and other repositories, provided insight into the process that produced consequential decisions.

From these materials came a picture of governmental abuse of power, use of secret informants, and the behind-the-scenes role of Justice Felix Frankfurter. I wondered how the Founding Fathers, who created a republic to provide freedoms that were unavailable under colonial rule, would have felt about the suppression of political dissent by the legislative, executive, and judicial branches they designed. Then there was the complicity of the academy. Two other Michigan professors, who relied on the Fifth Amendment, received sanctions out of the same campus investigation. Moreover, the university abetted the government to sabotage the careers of left-wing graduate students. Michigan was far from unique in these undertakings.[3]

Today many Americans view McCarthyism as a one-time aberration. Yet, from time to time, current events evoke temptations to sacrifice rights in hope for security. Such was the case in late 2015 when a wave of terrorist attacks was followed by Islamophobic proposals. In his winter commencement address that year, University of Michigan president Mark Schlissel urged graduates to consider the parallel to the actions taken in 1954 against Davis and his colleagues: "I hope you can apply the lessons learned from the mistakes made by both our nation and our university during the McCarthy Era."[4]

One objective of this book is to provide a fuller record of the treatment of Chandler Davis by the United States government and the University of Michigan. Materials that were secret for many years inform this account. Analyses of crucial court cases reveal the respective roles that jurisprudence and chance played in determining ultimate outcomes. I also include links to Chandler's testimony before the House Un-American Activities Committee and the controversial Supreme Court ruling that decided his case.

Chandler's family: sister Mina in her mother Marian's lap, Chandler, sister Dorothy, and father Horace. (COURTESY OF NATALIE ZEMON DAVIS)

CHAPTER ONE

Red Diaper Baby

In 1953, Horace Chandler Davis was an instructor[1] in the mathematics department at the University of Michigan.[2] On November 10, Davis received a visit in his office from Donald Appell, an investigator for the House Un-American Activities Committee (HUAC). The meeting was brief. Appell began to discuss information HUAC had obtained linking Davis to the Communist Party in the United States (CPUSA).[3] Davis declined to answer questions, and Appell served him with a subpoena to testify at a HUAC subcommittee hearing planned for early in the following year. Over the next week Appell made visits, with court orders, to at least four other faculty at the University of Michigan.

All five of the professors were early in their careers with prior CPUSA affiliations. For example, biologist Clement Markert was a former CPUSA member who had fought with the Abraham Lincoln Brigade in the Spanish Civil War. These activities were long past. Markert was then receiving favorable consideration from his colleagues for promotion to associate professor. The subpoenas would have profound effects on everyone's career. Derailed was the promotion case of Markert as well as for lecturer

Lawrence Klein, who would later win the Nobel Prize for his pioneering work in econometrics.

The Michigan faculty responded to HUAC in different ways. Only Klein chose to cooperate. Davis, who had recently left the CPUSA, was intimately acquainted with the hazards his continuing political activity posed to an academic career.[4] As a so-called red diaper baby, his Communist parents had lost a number of jobs, contributing to a peripatetic childhood. At the time of Chandler's HUAC subpoena, his father, Horace Bancroft Davis, was in the process of being dismissed from a tenured position as associate professor of economics at the University of Kansas City. The review of the elder Davis came about when, a few months earlier, he refused to answer questions at a hearing of HUAC's cousin, the Senate Internal Security Subcommittee. In December Horace Davis was fired, again.

Chandler's parents, Horace and Marian Rubins Davis, met as graduate students at Columbia. They were kindred spirits who quickly fell in love. Both Horace and Marian were influenced by the liberal political stances of family members. Marian's father owned a furniture business in Minneapolis where, despite outside pressure, he welcomed unionization into his shop. Harry Winfield Rubins was generous with social welfare organizations, read *The New Republic*, and opposed the U.S. entry into the First World War. Marian graduated from Smith, where she was exposed to the writings of Marx. She began graduate work in economics at Columbia in 1922, open to, but not yet embracing, radical beliefs.

Horace was influenced by his Quaker mother's pacifism. He interrupted his undergraduate education at Harvard to join a Quaker mission in France during the First World War. After returning to the United States, he, with his mother, actively supported a textile workers' strike in Massachusetts. Completing an undergraduate degree at Harvard, Horace started work on a PhD in labor economics at Columbia. In his second year, as Marian began her study, Horace was in Geneva attempting to broaden his perspective through a position with the League of Nations' International Labor Organization. Working next in a Pittsburgh steel mill solidified his sympathies on the labor side of labor economics. Returning to Columbia to teach and continue work on his degree, Horace met Marian. They married in 1925.

Neither Davis had completed their doctorates when the opportunity arose for Horace to replace a labor economist on leave from Cornell. Marian secured a position as a research assistant to another faculty member. As the couple was nearing the end of their year in Ithaca, Chandler was born, on August 12, 1926. Marian subordinated her career ambitions to those of Horace, who had obtained a graduate fellowship permitting him to travel. Over the next two years, the family lived among and observed conditions for the working class in England, Wales, France, and Germany. The deprivation was striking.

A revelatory experience for Marian was the sight of starving children at a British market diving into tall trash cans to frantically scrounge for scraps. Horace reflected that their time "in Europe gave us a view of the poverty there and started us on the way to joining the Communist Party."[5] The effect of European living on the infant Chandler manifested itself in his language. His first words were in French. German gave way to English.

Chandler's earliest memories date to after the family's return from Europe. With a final year of fellowship support, they moved to Pittsburgh in 1928. Renewing his prior labor connections, Horace immediately found himself in the middle of a rebellion within the United Mine Workers. A Communist-led faction was attempting to break off and form a new union. As the year went on, Horace observed, at close range, grievances of steel and mine workers. In the process he and Marian established relationships with young University of Pittsburgh faculty involved in the establishment of an American Civil Liberties Union (ACLU) chapter in the city.

When a liberal University of Pittsburgh student group organized a rally in support of two unjustly imprisoned labor figures, Thomas Mooney and Warren Billings, the Davises were among the enthusiastic backers. Efforts by the university to suppress the student organization were documented by Horace in a critical article that appeared in *The New Republic*. The piece, titled "Academic Freedom in Pittsburgh," was not the sort of press a university desires. [6]

Having a pro-labor reputation could be a serious impediment on the academic job market. University administrators depended on the support of business-minded trustees. Horace was attracted by an opening to lead a long-term survey on unemployment in the Pittsburgh area. Not only was he well qualified, with an influential recommendation for the post, but the work would have provided his nomadic family with the stability of several more years in Pittsburgh. The survey, however, was under the control of the University of Pittsburgh, and Horace's nomination could not pass the chancellor. With meager options for employment in 1929, Horace accepted a faculty position at a denominational college in Memphis, Southwestern (now Rhodes) College.

Even without foreknowledge of the challenges that would arise out of the coming Depression, the Davises could be seen as a poor fit for Southwestern. Atheists with strong values in civil rights and equal opportunity were entering a religious, segregated culture. The plight of Black tenant farmers was a shock to their sensibilities.

Conflicts arose immediately at the college. Horace was assigned to teach a remedial course where the objective was to raise the level of the students so that they could begin the regular curriculum. For a text Horace selected *Introduction to Reflective Thinking*. [7] The Columbia faculty-produced book delved into instances where scholars such as Copernicus and Darwin had struggled against entrenched dogma. With an analysis of the Bible that was certain to arouse controversy, the president instructed Horace to find a different text.

One shared faculty responsibility proved unbearable for Horace: leading chapel. When his turn came to deliver a sermon

Horace tried his best, but it became clear to both himself and the administration that he was unsuited for the responsibility. Memphis would be another one-year residence for the Davises. As he served out his time, the effects of the Depression on the local economy became apparent. For at least Marian, the Communist Party seemed the only solution to the problems of American society. She joined. For Horace, it would take more time.

The Davises' last week in Memphis was eventful. Several labor organizers had been arrested recently in Atlanta for leading an integrated rally. Marian and Horace set out to arrange an integrated Memphis meeting demonstrating solidarity with their imprisoned comrades. To publicize the protest they distributed leaflets, and Marian answered questions posed by a reporter.

Her interview appeared in the local newspaper on the morning of the scheduled rally. Fallout was immediate, beginning with crank telephone calls. A tearful Chandler was sent home by the mother of a neighborhood playmate with a message for his parents to get him "a [Black child] to play with."[8] Horace and Marian were arrested and held overnight. A rally without the Davises, who managed to leave Memphis safely a few days afterward, was held surreptitiously among emboldened African American residents. Eighty-five years later Chandler had no memory of the incident,[9] but for a child just learning to read, the effect must have been significant.

The next residence of the Davis family, 1930–1933, was in the Sunnyside neighborhood of Queens, New York. There, Horace divided his labor between work on a thesis and writing articles for a left-wing news service, the Federated Press. Monetary support for these endeavors was furnished by Horace's mother.

For Chandler, who spent ages four to seven in Sunnyside, it was the most stable period of his childhood. His experiences included a sizable dose of CPUSA culture. Horace had joined Marian in the CPUSA, and they became particularly active members. As Sunnyside was home to a substantial number of other Communists, many household visitors were from the CPUSA. Rather than participating in traditional scout groups, Chandler became a member of the CPUSA-affiliated Young Pioneers.

After three years in Sunnyside, Horace's doctoral thesis on living conditions for steel workers was accepted by the Columbia economics department. Academic jobs in the Depression mid-1930s were scarce. Horace's only domestic opportunity was a part-time position at the New School for Social Science. At the close of the summer, he was recruited for the faculty at an evening college for adults that was just opening in São Paulo.[10] Within a couple of weeks, Chandler and his younger sisters joined their parents on a ship for the voyage to Brazil.

As at Southwestern College, Horace was assuming a position with the prospect for long-term employment. Unlike in Memphis, the Davis family became happily ensconced in their new surroundings. Nonetheless, the outcome was effectively the same. The college board decided against renewing Horace's contract for a second year.

It can be difficult for an individual to ascertain the actual reason behind his or her termination. Horace speculated that his fate was sealed early on when he was assigned to deliver a series of lectures on charged topics, including Fascism and Communism. Unquestionably the views he expressed were not in step with the Brazilian establishment. Yet Horace was a forthright individual whose opinions were often out of the mainstream. Later, Chandler would diagnose his father's difficulties in holding employment to his being "too Red."[11] Indeed, Horace's political views seemed to override his teaching, scholarship, and credential of a Columbia PhD.

The next stop on the academic job circuit for the Davis family was Bradford Junior College, a women's school in Massachusetts, north of Boston. Arriving with a three-year contract, Horace brought undesirable notoriety to the college when he was picked up by the police for selling pamphlets condemning the anti-Semitic figure Father Coughlin. He was fired at the end of his second year after attempting, at a public hearing, to obtain the use of a municipal auditorium for a CPUSA function.

In 1936 Horace joined the economics department at Simmons College in Boston. The position included several seemingly attractive features. Members of the Simmons faculty and administration held a range of left-wing views.[12] Marian was appointed to teach statistics. After five years of teaching, Horace was informed of his termination by the college president. As Chandler was beginning college at Harvard, his father was zero for four in the academy.

Teenage Chandler and sister Mina.

CHAPTER TWO

CPUSA → reformist

Risky Behavior

Most of the developments in this book were driven by the vastly different perceptions that Americans held of the CPUSA. For Horace and Marian Davis, the CPUSA was a movement to rescue American workers and African Americans from an oppressive and discriminatory socioeconomic system. To many others in the United States, the CPUSA was a sinister, Moscow-orchestrated conspiracy dedicated to the overthrow, by any means, of the American way. Over subsequent decades opportunistic politicians would exploit the Cold War to stoke fears about the CPUSA and its activities. As we shall see, the portrayal of the CPUSA as an existential threat would place its members in serious jeopardy.

how?

Not all red diaper babies followed in the political tracks of their parents.[1] Chandler embraced the CPUSA early on, assimilating into the network of CPUSA family friends in Queens. His formal education began there in the public schools. By learning Portuguese, he was able to continue his studies in São Paulo.

The next family move was in 1934 to the shoe-manufacturing town of Haverhill, Massachusetts. Chandler's elementary school

performance over the two years was mixed. His obvious precoc-
ity resulted in advancement over several grades. Meanwhile his
misbehavior was a problem. Several trips to the principal's office
had little effect.

For his parents' positions at Simmons College, Chandler relocated with them to the Boston suburbs. Well ahead of his age
group in school, his secondary education would continue at a
normal pace. During this period in Newton, the behavioral problems evaporated, and his strong scholarship persisted. It was also
a time of major developments for members of the CPUSA.

In the 1930s, some Americans were attracted to the CPUSA
by its opposition to the Fascist movement, which was to some
degree tolerated in the United States. A dilemma for these members arose in 1939 with the completion of the German-Soviet
Non-Aggression Pact. Unable to reconcile the collusion of the
Soviet Union with the Nazis, some left the CPUSA. Two years
later, Hitler's invasion of Soviet territory restored the CPUSA-
alignment to its opposition of the Fascists.

The Davis family, with its pacifist leanings, was undeterred by
the Pact. They viewed the arrangement as a positive step away
from war. When Soviet casualties began in 1941, Marion volun-
teered considerable energy to the Russian war-relief effort.

After his firing from Simmons College, Horace elected to
pursue a non-academic position. In Haverhill he had col-
lected data for a book on shoe workers.[2] The research brought
him into contact with leaders of the union, the United Shoe
Workers. Horace's book, *Shoes: The Workers and the Industry*,
appeared around the time of his firing from Simmons. These circumstances made Horace a natural fit for the recently vacated
position as director of research for the United Shoe Workers.
A difficulty was that the family move to the Washington, DC,
suburbs came with Chandler one semester shy of graduation.
An arrangement was made for him to board with neighbors in
Newton during his remaining months of high school.

Just after turning sixteen, Chandler entered Harvard on a

prestigious Harvard National Scholarship. In his 1942 choice of college, Chandler was not only following in the footsteps of his father but a number of paternal ancestors who had attended Harvard and Radcliffe.[3] For many freshmen, college is a broadening experience where they encounter people of other races, religions, and nationalities. In particular, students are often exposed to more radical political views than were available to them in their high schools and communities. Unlike his peers, Chandler grew up in a household where the *Daily Worker* was a fixture. Even so, at Harvard he developed friendships with individuals holding distinctly different far-left orientations, including Trotskyists and non-Marxists.

Paralleling the influence of Harvard life on Chandler's intellectual development was his immersion in the science-fiction community.[4] In high school he became an avid reader of *Astounding Science-Fiction* magazine and began attending fan club meetings in the Boston area. Several years later, Chandler would become a prominent author of the genre, but by his freshman year of college he was already an active participant in the subculture of devotees. Again, a broad spectrum of political views was represented.

After his first year of college, Chandler joined his family, now living in Cumberland, a western Maryland town near the West Virginia border. Horace was working for the CIO trade union. With an extended summer break due to the war, Chandler took a job in a textile factory. Over this period, he joined the CPUSA. Rather than being a life-altering move, becoming a member of the CPUSA was a natural transition for Chandler. When asked three-quarters of a century later about the factors motivating him to join the CPUSA in 1943, he replied that "it was just what I had been expecting to do all my life."[5] The toll that political activity had taken on his father's career was no deterrent, nor would he ever regret having held a CPUSA membership card, even as the risks accelerated over the next decade.

The stint in the CPUSA was short-lived. In September, Chandler returned to a Harvard in full mobilization to support the war effort. During the spring Harvard had become one of several American colleges to institute a Navy V-12 training program. The purpose of this one-year campus program was to prepare students for duty as officers in the military. Over the summer nearly a thousand students, drawn from inside and outside the university, enrolled in the Harvard V-12 program. Participants became members of the Naval Reserve. They pursued a curriculum that included both university and naval courses taken while in uniform and under military discipline. Chandler, anxious to do his part to fight Hitler, enlisted in the V-12 program at the end of 1943. Following standard practice for Party members, Chandler simultaneously resigned from the CPUSA.   Navy - Army - AF - M

Throughout 1944 Chandler underwent a grueling regimen of course overloads and military training that would allow him to graduate early in 1945 with a major in mathematics. One of his classes was an advanced course covering topics selected by the professor, George David Birkhoff. Birkhoff, who was in the last year of his life, was the greatest American mathematician up to this time. He took a special interest in Chandler.

In the spring term of 1945, Chandler entered Midshipmen's School, receiving his commission as an ensign in June. He then served on a minesweeper in Florida until his honorable discharge nine months after the war ended. While on active duty, Chandler tried his hand as a science-fiction author. One of his stories was accepted, making him a published author when he entered graduate school at Harvard in 1946.

Chandler's interests were in both mathematics and physics. Although formally admitted to the mathematics department, his first year of graduate courses more closely resembled the schedule of a physics student. In the second year he returned to mathematics. Chandler expected to take more physics later, but this plan did not materialize.

As a graduate student, Chandler rejoined the CPUSA. While strict secrecy was maintained with almost all memberships, a few individuals served openly and proselytized the Party view. Chandler requested to serve in this public role but was turned down by the local hierarchy. The reason given to him was that his views were not sufficiently faithful to the Party-line Marxist orthodoxy.

It turned out that the CPUSA's efforts at confidentiality were no match for the aggressive tactics of the FBI. A Freedom of Information Act request has revealed that the FBI became aware of Chandler's CPUSA membership within six months of his return to Harvard for graduate study.[6] One source for the information was a list of Cambridge student members that the FBI clandestinely obtained from the New England CPUSA headquarters office in Boston.[7] Confirmation was provided by the discovery of Chandler's 1946 membership card in garbage from the apartment of the secretary-treasurer of the New England CPUSA.[8]

Although disappointed that he was not authorized to serve as an open member, Chandler found stimulation in his interactions with the other graduate students in his CPUSA branch. Consistent with his own anti-nuclear beliefs and the CPUSA practice of having members become active in less controversial organizations pursuing complementary objectives, Chandler joined the Federation of American Scientists. The mission of the organization, founded by scientists from the Manhattan Project, was to promote international control and peaceful use of atomic energy. Chandler, and the CPUSA, were particularly enthusiastic about the Federation's advocacy of a pledge against first use of nuclear weapons.

Involvement with another CPUSA-approved organization introduced Chandler to his future wife. In 1948 the Progressive Party was created, in large part, to support the presidential candidacy of Henry Wallace. Its platform, including conciliation with the Soviet Union and desegregation, was attractive to members of the CPUSA. At a meeting of the

Party's youth wing, the Young Progressives, Chandler met another member, Natalie Zemon.[9] She was a senior at Smith College who was at Harvard to participate in a summer program on the philosophy of science.

Chandler arrived at the Young Progressives meeting after playing Ping-Pong. Seventy years later his appearance with a paddle under his arm remained vivid for Natalie.[10] Holding political views compatible with Chandler's, she had already interacted with people from the radical left. The men always left her with the impression that their doctrinal commitments superseded any interest in more "normal activities" that she enjoyed, such as tennis.[11] Seeing a "handsome" man with other potentially appealing qualities, Natalie took the initiative to reach out and begin a conversation with Chandler.

Chandler and Natalie quickly learned that they shared a deep interest in a broad array of intellectual pursuits as well as normal activities. Within a few weeks, they decided to marry. That Chandler was an atheist and Natalie Jewish was of no consequence for them or for Chandler's parents. Natalie's parents were another matter. Her mother, especially, was resolutely opposed to Natalie marrying a non-Jewish man.

Natalie Zemon was born in Detroit on November 8, 1928. Despite the vicissitudes of the Depression, her father, Julian, was a prosperous merchant supplying textiles to the automobile industry. His marriage to Helen Lamport created a household that maintained a strong Jewish identity without observing Kosher or other strict practices. The Zemon social life was concentrated around people and activities at a Jewish country club.

Natalie was an outstanding student with a drive to excel. She was admitted to an elite private high school for women, Kingswood, located on a beautiful campus in the Detroit suburbs. The typical Kingswood student came from a wealthy Christian family. Natalie was selected within the quota of two Jews per class. She thrived at the school, embracing a curriculum rich in history and literature.

Contrasted with her happy assimilation into the culture at Kingswood where she became student council president, Natalie felt uncomfortable among her Jewish peers at the country club. She was appalled by the materialism and ostentation among these *nouveau riche* families. Her ambitions were to succeed and to benefit the world.

In the fall of 1945, just after the end of the Second World War, Natalie entered Smith College. She recalls that the scene she found herself in was full of "exhilaration" and "hope of remaking Europe and the world, but some worry of what was going to happen with the bomb."[12] Optimism, however, was the predominant feeling with the utopian desire of her generation to "mak[e] the world a better place. Now is our chance."

Natalie always loved to learn. At Smith her worldview was greatly expanded by two other women. "Marxist socialism was a revelation when I heard about it in my freshman year from Judy Mogil, herself fresh from Music and Art High School and all the sophistication of New York City. Here was a solution to the ferocious competition that set one individual against the other; here was a way to obliterate crass materialism and allow people to enjoy the work they did."[13] Mogil became a lifelong friend.

A sophomore-year course on the Renaissance and Reformation taught by Leona Gabel kindled Natalie's fascination with early modern history. She began to read primary sources leading to honors work under the direction of Gabel. The topic that Natalie chose for her thesis was the sixteenth-century heretical philosopher Pietro Pomponazzi.

By the time of her summer 1948 study at Harvard, Natalie had moved further from her parents than either party realized. She and Chandler found, in each other, the individual with whom they wanted to spend their lives. The Zemons urged a one-year separation. Seeing no feasible compromise, Chandler and Natalie decided to marry secretly. When her parents learned of the union shortly afterward, they severed all relations except to pay Natalie's tuition for her senior year. It would take many years for an even partial reconciliation between mother and daughter.

Graduating from Smith in 1949, Natalie joined Chandler at Harvard. Officially a graduate student in history at Radcliffe, Natalie took courses at Harvard. There she studied early modern British history with W. K. Jordan. Meanwhile, Chandler completed his thesis "Lattices of Modal Operators," nominally under the direction of Garrett Birkhoff, the son of George David Birkhoff.

Near the end of his graduate study, Chandler began to experience fallout from his CPUSA membership.[14] In advance of his final year, as the Harvard National Scholarship depleted, Chandler applied for an Atomic Energy Commission Fellowship. These fellowships, created one year earlier in 1948, were designed to support students in fields of science that were contributing to atomic energy research. As a reference for his application, Chandler provided the name of MIT mathematician Dirk Struik, whom he originally met through his parents. Struik was a longtime Communist, and he was under surveillance by the FBI.

Apparently Struik's telephone was wiretapped because Chandler's FBI files include summaries of his conversations with Struik. Of particular interest was a courtesy call in which Chandler informed Struik of the fellowship application.[15] Seeing some possibility of Struik's connection to an atomic energy project, the FBI put together the information in its Chandler files so that it would be available for the Director to disseminate to the Atomic Energy Commission.[16] The profile of a young CPUSA scientist engaged in this area of research called for a formal report.[17]

Despite the FBI's efforts to intervene, Chandler's Atomic Energy Commission application was successful. However, an open member of the CPUSA, physics graduate student Hans Freistadt, had been a recipient of the fellowship in the year prior to Chandler. His award became the subject of a political battle between Senator Bourke Hickenlooper and the Atomic Energy Commission. Among the outcomes were Freistadt's loss of the fellowship and the instigation of a non-Communist affidavit for awardees.

The summer 1949 affidavit requirement placed Chandler in a bind. He recalled: "I discussed with my [CPUSA] branch whether it would be best to drop out at least temporarily so I could honestly sign the oath, but the group decision was that I should stay in the Party and scrounge around for other funds, and I did."[18] The result was that "in 1949–50 I remember that Natalie & I did have to draw down our savings to zero."[19]

Chandler faced another conflict between politics, principles, and career when he reached the job market in 1950. At first it appeared he had been spared the burden of submitting applications when his advisor, on his own initiative, secured a position for Chandler at UCLA. However, the University of California had a decade-long prohibition of Communists from their faculty. Chandler may or may not have been aware of the ban. What he did know was that in 1949 the California Board of Regents instituted a loyalty oath under which university employees were expected to sign a pledge that they were not members of the Communist Party.[20] The new policy led to a bitter, protracted battle between faculty and the Regents. Some non-Communist faculty refused to sign the oath based on principles such as academic freedom.

As Chandler entered the fray in February 1950, University of California faculty received an ultimatum with a deadline to sign the oath or be dismissed. In considering his options, Chandler reasoned that "in this situation even if I had left the Party I would not have been willing to sign the oath, because it would have been a breach of solidarity with the courageous resistance to it."[21] Over the next few months, however, mediation attempts by alumni offered some hope of mitigating the oath. When, by May, the efforts had led to only minor modifications in the policy, Chandler resigned from UCLA. He was fortunate to obtain, on short notice, a mathematics instructorship at the University of Michigan. The University of California battle would continue over the next several years with resignations, firings, litigation, changes in the oath, and some reinstatements)

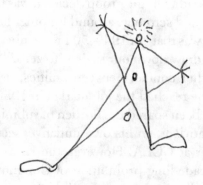

J. Edgar Hoover, 1925.

CHAPTER THREE

The CPUSA and the United States Government

Chandler's membership in the CPUSA subjected him to the scrutiny of the FBI and HUAC. Concerns in the United States government about Communism date back to the time of the 1917 Bolshevik Revolution. Coincidentally, a few months before this event in Russia, twenty-two-year-old J. Edgar Hoover, just graduated from George Washington Law School, began his career at the FBI (called the Bureau of Investigation until 1935).[1] There, as he rose rapidly through the ranks, Hoover would engage in a campaign against Communism that would shape government action and influence popular sentiment.

With the country in the midst of the First World War, Hoover's first Bureau of Investigation assignment was as a clerk in a section working on the deportation of alien anarchists. Hoover oversaw the investigations by Bureau agents to identify suspects and collated the paperwork required for further action. As anti-subversion laws with names featuring Espionage, Sedition, and Immigration took effect, he and his associates expanded their purview to radicals that included Bolsheviks, while broadening their attention to citizens.[2]

Fervently committed to carrying out these tasks, Hoover was soon promoted, about the time of the Armistice, from clerk to a Justice Department attorney.

In 1919 Hoover's Justice Department mentor, A. Mitchell Palmer, became Attorney General. Meanwhile, the end of the war brought considerable labor and racial unrest, arousing public concerns.[3] After a number of mysterious bombings, including of his own home, Palmer created a Radical Division (later named the General Investigation Division),[4] headed by Hoover, in the Bureau of Investigation. The mission of the division became to identify and keep tabs on radicals, including Communists, both alien and native.

Under his new authority, Hoover instituted an upgrade in information technology. He had worked his way through law school by cataloguing new acquisitions at the Library of Congress. Now, for the Radical Division, he developed an elaborate filing system of index cards and folders with intelligence on suspected radical individuals and their groups.

A major problem for Hoover was a lack of statutory tools for prosecuting radicals. The Espionage and Sedition Acts were restricted to time of war and the Immigration Act of 1918 to aliens, leaving no basis for locking up radical citizens. Nor did Hoover have clear authority for his aggressive surveillance of Americans. Both Palmer and a Senate committee had recommended passage of a peacetime sedition law. In what would not be the last brazen move of his career, Hoover proceeded with the expectation that a sedition law would soon be enacted.[5] With a network of agents and informants operating under a low standard of evidence, he oversaw the opening and maintenance of thousands of files. No sedition law was enacted at this time.

One month after Hoover took the reins of the Radical Division came a milestone in the turbulent history of the CPUSA. In early September 1919, the Communist Party of America and the Communist Labor Party came into existence and waged an acrimonious struggle for a claim to the first authentic Communist franchise in the United States.[6] Most of their 25,000 to 40,000 members were foreign-born and had previously belonged to some faction of a socialist party or to the Industrial Workers of the World (IWW), a left-wing labor group.

The two Communist organizations drew the interest of Hoover. Bureau agents attended their founding conventions in Chicago.[7] They then infiltrated the local chapters, providing Hoover with member names and Party literature for his files. The large bodies of immigrants with radical views were ideal Hoover targets for deportation.

While the Radical Division identified the undesirable aliens, the Immigration Act of 1918 placed the actual deportations under the auspices of the Labor Department and its immigration officials. In response to a September 1919 overture from Palmer, Secretary of Labor William Wilson agreed to a collaboration among their agencies for enforcing the statute.[8] Hoover and his Justice Department colleagues then met with like-minded Labor counterparts to strategize mass deportation roundups that would become known as the Palmer Raids. Despite the Palmer name and the Labor Department's *de jure* authority, Hoover would be the architect and the impetus behind the initiative.[9]

On January 2, 1920, thousands of people were arrested in raids of the two Communist parties in cities across the country. The *New York Times* reported enthusiastically on these operations, editorializing three days later that the Justice Department had "planned with shrewdness and a large wisdom, and carried out with extraordinary success the nabbing of nearly four thousand radicals . . . all working for the destruction of the Government of the United States."

Adjudication of the cases brought closer review of the Justice Department procedures during the raids. Two developments in particular would change the perception of the Palmer Raids. In

March, Assistant Secretary of Labor Louis Post replaced an ailing William Wilson as the Labor point person. Second, for a habeus corpus hearing of detainees from the Boston raid, Federal Judge George Anderson solicited the participation of Harvard law professors Felix Frankfurter and Zechariah Chafee. Post, Frankfurter, and Chafee were sensitive to the civil liberties and due process protections of both citizens and aliens. They soon uncovered serious abuses in the conduct of the Justice Department.

The raids were planned to maximize the number of arrests and deportations.[10] To assure the former, the Bureau of Investigation instructed its infiltrators to act as *agents provocateurs*, arranging chapter meetings for the scheduled time of the raid. Hoover was provided with blank warrants that were completed after arrest and questioning. Many of those detained were citizens or innocent bystanders. Suspects, denied access to attorneys, were coerced into making confessions. For many refusing to admit that they were radical aliens, excessive bail was imposed in the hopes that indefinite detention would break down resistance.

With Post battling to reassert the role that Justice had usurped from Labor, most of the cases evaporated.[11] Frankfurter and Chafee collaborated with ten other distinguished legal authorities to document their discoveries for the National Public Government League (NPGL) in a scathing pamphlet titled "We the American People: Report Upon the Illegal Practices of the United States Department of Justice."

Hoover reacted with what would become his modus operandi in dealing with opponents: He directed his agents to conduct confidential investigations of Post and the NPGL.[12] No dirt was found, and an attempt to impeach Post was unsuccessful. All the while, Palmer raised fears of a major Communist uprising for May Day that failed to materialize.[13] Public and government concerns about Communism subsequently abated. The period 1919–1920 became known as the time of the first Red Scare in the United States.

Hoover's objective in ordering the January 2 raids, to expel the bulk of the two Communist parties, went unrealized. Out of an estimated 10,000 arrests, just 556 resulted in deportations.[14] Nevertheless, there were damaging consequences for Communism in America. After the raids, the Communist Party and the Communist Labor Party found it expedient to shift their operations underground. The secrecy gave the brand a sinister aura and was accompanied by a drastic drop in membership.[15] Over the next few years, splits and mergers took place in the American organizations as they competed for the imprimatur of the Communist International (Comintern) in Moscow. The 10,000 or so remaining Communists in the United States then came together, aboveground, under one (changing) name, and Comintern direction.[16]

In 1921 President Warren Harding headed a Republican changeover in power. Hoover survived the transition by deflecting blame for the by then unpopular Palmer Raids to their namesake.[17] Otherwise, Harding appointed cronies to his cabinet who embarked on a variety of unscrupulous endeavors. Adapting to the new culture, Hoover was soon promoted to Assistant Director of the Bureau of Investigation, even learning techniques from his new associates for dealing with enemies. When Congress began investigating corruption in the Harding administration, one of its targets, Attorney General Harry Daughtery, authorized break-ins by the Bureau to the offices of the troublesome congressmen.[18] In comparison, Hoover's prior surveillance abuses, such as obtaining bank account information on the NPGL and confidential records from military intelligence on Post, were of a lesser degree. But Hoover would prove to be an apt learner.

Revelations of executive branch corruption and the collusive abuses by the Justice Department and Bureau of Investigation emerged after the 1923 death of Harding. President Calvin Coolidge replaced Attorney General Daugherty with reformer Harlan Fiske Stone. Director William Burns took the fall for the Bureau of Investigation's malfeasance. Stone forced out Burns, abolished the General Investigation Division, and instructed the Bureau to cease its political surveillance and to focus on criminal activity.[19]

Ironically, Stone's choice for Burns's replacement to direct the Bureau of Intelligence, J. Edgar Hoover, had a sweet tooth for surveillance and a powerful disdain for political dissidents. In their interview, Hoover impressed Stone as a person of character who would observe the prescribed boundaries for investigations.[20] The future Supreme Court Chief Justice made an erroneous judgment. While substantially reducing his corps of informants to appear to comply with Stone's order, Hoover continued to augment his files with intelligence received more passively through already established outside channels.[21]

As attorneys general came and went, what Hoover craved was a law that would enable his Bureau to surveil, and the Department of Justice to prosecute, Communists and other radicals.[22] Over the years, Congress had flirted with such legislation. In 1919, a Senate special committee, chaired by North Carolina Democrat Lee Overman, recommended reinstatement of the type of sedition laws that had recently expired with the end of the First World War.[23] Then, in 1930, the House Special Committee to Investigate Communist Activities, under Republican Hamilton Fish III of New York, proposed to legalize the Bureau of Investigation's surveillance of Communists. This never-enacted legislation was opposed by Hoover due to its absence of any criminal penalties for subversive activity.[24]

Roosevelt 1936

Eventually, in 1936, President Franklin Roosevelt began secretly authorizing Hoover to employ some of the investigative techniques of Communism that he had been carrying out for nearly two decades.[25] CPUSA membership, however, still did not violate any federal law. Some delegates of Congress continued to press their anti-Communist agenda.

What would become HUAC was born on May 26, 1938, when the House of Representatives voted 191–41 in favor of a resolution by Martin Dies.[26] The proposal of the Texas Democrat was to establish a special committee to investigate "the extent, character, and object of un-American propaganda activities in the United States." *Dies Committee*

Dies was a right-winger who held labor unions, foreigners, and Communists in contempt. The resolution's success, and its phraseology, owed much to New York Democrat Samuel Dickstein, a vehement anti-fascist.[27] Dickstein had previously gone after Nazi sympathizers with legislation that euphemistically referred to "un-American activities" and "un-American propaganda."[28] When Dies appropriated Dickstein's verbiage, he gained an improbable ally in Dickstein who held a very different un-American target in mind. In any event, the endorsements by Dies and Dickstein won support from different wings of the Democratic Party as well as Republicans.

Dies was selected to chair the special committee, which would receive annual renewals until it was made permanent in 1945. Originally referred to as the Dies Committee, it is now remembered as HUAC (House Un-American Activities Committee). At its outset, the Dies Committee showed interest in both fascists and Communists, but the choices of its chair and members, such as John Rankin and J. Parnell Thomas rather than Dickstein, ensured that HUAC's principal focus would be Communism.

Under Dies, the committee embarked on hearings where they berated leftists. HUAC members denounced the New Deal and labor organizations for their alleged associations with the CPUSA. The Dies Committee provided good copy for the press. Moreover, the timing, with Hitler's aggression in Europe and the 1939 pact with Russia, made Communism an easy mark.

The prewar mood in the United States was ripe for the sort of sedition laws that had failed over the past twenty years. In 1939 Representative Howard Smith of Virginia bundled together several prior unsuccessful measures, which, after amendment by others, would pass overwhelmingly in 1940. The Smith Act prohibited certain activities, including for an individual to advocate, or to organize with others, a group that advocates the overthrow of the United States government by force or violence, as well as conspiracy to organize such a group.[29]

Membership in the CPUSA was not explicitly a violation of the Smith Act, but some of the law's supporters saw it as an avenue for prosecuting Communists. In the Smith Act's early years, with Russia becoming an ally of the United States in 1941, indictments were primarily restricted to Trotskyists and fascists. Then, around the end of the Second World War, American attitudes toward Communism began shifting again. Stalin was working to consolidate the Soviet bloc, and the Cold War was ramping up. Over the next several years current events, together with their usage in American politics, gave rise to a second, and more consequential, Red Scare in the United States.

To begin with, President Truman was politically vulnerable as he faced American discontent over postwar labor strikes and shortages of meat and household goods. Winston Churchill, in his famous March 1946 speech at Westminster College in Missouri, called out the Soviet Union for its creation of an "iron curtain." Later in the year a political newcomer, Richard Nixon, defeated a veteran Democratic incumbent to win a California congressional seat. Nixon's campaign tactics included smearing his opponent with specious allegations of Communist associations.[30] Meanwhile, Joseph McCarthy of Wisconsin won election to the Senate. Overall, in the 1946 midterm elections Republican contentions that Democrats were soft on Communism helped the party gain control of both chambers of Congress.

For HUAC the new Republican congressional majority meant more than the change in chairs from John Wood to J. Parnell Thomas. When the Democrats were in control, the Southern-dominated HUAC found its Communist-hunting endeavors out of favor with the president and the mainstream of the ruling party. In 1947 HUAC's unchanged agenda would be fully in line with the platform of the majority Republican Party. The committee moved from the margin to some level of credibility.

Chairman Thomas targeted the Hollywood motion picture industry for HUAC's Communist investigation in 1947. The choice proved to be well suited for his purposes. Whether or not the Red influence manifested itself in movies as Thomas believed, there were indeed a significant number of CPUSA members on both sides of the camera. Moreover, nobody aroused greater interest in the American public than a movie star. The committee had always been keen for publicity. Testimonies by matinee idols were certain to dominate the print media and newsreels. It remained to ferret out the, once again, underground Communists.

HUAC, however, lacked the investigative resources and files of the FBI. In preparation for the Hollywood hearings, Chairman Thomas met with J. Edgar Hoover to propose an alliance. Since the days of Dies, HUAC and the FBI had, in effect, been in a turf battle to be the government agency that kept the CPUSA in line.[31] President Roosevelt had a clear favorite in the competition. Thomas's view that "it seems as though the New Deal was hand in glove with the Communist Party"[32] conveyed the sentiments of his colleagues on the committee. Roosevelt found himself increasingly relying on the obliging Hoover, both to surveil the CPUSA and to monitor HUAC.[33]

For his part, the fiercely territorial Hoover had been reluctant to cooperate with HUAC for fear of it compromising his sources and (sometimes illegal) methods.[34] On the other hand, with decisions on the scope of the Smith Act up in the air, Hoover was frustrated by the inability to prosecute the CPUSA activity the FBI uncovered. The prospect of HUAC publicly exposing the Communists was appealing to him, provided it could be accomplished without revealing any FBI fingerprints. The decision of Hoover, at their meeting on June 24, 1947, to share information covertly with Thomas had enormous ramifications. HUAC immediately received leads and intelligence, including copies of membership cards that the FBI had obtained in prior clandestine break-ins of the CPUSA's Los Angeles office.[35] Not only would Thomas have a list of confirmed Communists for the Hollywood hearing, but HUAC would continue to receive information from FBI files in subsequent investigations.

HUAC announced subpoenas to forty-three individuals for the 1947 Washington hearings on "Communist Infiltration of the Motion Picture Industry."[36] Just under half were suspected of CPUSA membership. The witnesses, not all of whom testified, became designated as friendly or unfriendly depending upon whether they would cooperate with HUAC. The friendlies included studio heads Jack Warner, Louis B. Mayer, and Walt Disney as well as actors Gary Cooper and Ronald Reagan. Most of the unfriendlies were lesser-known screenwriters with Communist ties. A few were directors, and only one unfriendly, Larry Parks, was an actor.

The politics of many of Hollywood's celebrities tended toward the liberal New Deal camp. Reaction to the subpoenas was swift. A high-profile group, calling itself the Committee for the First Amendment, formed to protest what they viewed as an unconstitutional intrusion into political beliefs and an attempt to suppress free expression. Among its members were Humphrey Bogart, Lauren Bacall, and John Huston. These were people who understood publicity. They issued press releases and chartered a flight from Los Angeles to put their star power up against the hearings in Washington. The plane made stops in cities along the way to raise awareness. Some of those remaining in Hollywood produced radio programs critical of HUAC.

The October hearings took place before a HUAC subcommittee in the ornate Caucus Room of the Old House Office Building. The glamour of the movie stars was a magnet for spectators and the media. Newspaper reporters, radio announcers, microphones, newsreel and even a television camera (1947 was the year that commercial television made its debut) were present to transmit the words, images, and wardrobe of the celebrities.

Thomas's plan was to have friendlies testify first, revealing that the CPUSA was placing its propaganda into Hollywood movies. The actual testimony failed to make his case. Everyone did deplore Communism and acknowledged its threat to the country, many saying the CPUSA should be made an illegal organization.[37] The moguls, however, believed that the Communist presence in Hollywood was largely confined to a faction of screenwriters whose efforts to proselytize had been thwarted by the producers and their associates in the studio system. When it came to identifying particular movies that exhibited the Party line, only three examples were offered, each explainable by production during the period that Russia was a sympathetic ally of the United States.[38] With the vigilant studios effectively policing Communist propaganda, the investigation revealed no need for government intervention or censorship. Testimony of the movie stars, particularly Gary Cooper, lacked substance. The first week of the hearings came off as what they were, a publicity stunt.

In the second week, Thomas initiated what would become the signature tactic of HUAC, outing members of the CPUSA. From the FBI and other sources, the committee identified seventy-nine film industry workers as members of the CPUSA. Nineteen were subpoenaed to testify. Many were named as Communists in the testimony by the friendlies.

At the hearing the suspects would be asked what will be referred to here as the *Communist question*: "Are you now or have you ever been a member of the Communist Party?" The CPUSA witnesses had four undesirable options. They could deny or admit to membership, decline to answer asserting their Fifth Amendment rights against self-incrimination, or simply refuse to answer the question. An admission left the witness in jeopardy of job dismissal and of a subsequent Smith Act indictment. Unjustified refusal to answer would be followed with a contempt citation and prosecution. Taking the Fifth Amendment was generally regarded as protection against contempt, but it would be a few years until the Supreme Court definitively validated this course. In the meantime, HUAC, and possibly employers, would regard assertion of the Fifth Amendment as an admission. Denial called for rebuttal by the committee, making the membership cards from the illegal FBI raids vital pieces of evidence.

Two of the unfriendlies who were called to testify, Emmet Lavery and Bertolt Brecht, denied that they had ever been Communists. Brecht was subpoenaed because of his writings and his connections to Johannes and Gerhart Eisler whom HUAC believed were key figures in the Communist Party. Lavery, who was president of the Screen Writers Guild, had been publicly alleged to be a Communist, including in testimony by two friendlies. HUAC did not rebut the claims of Brecht and Lavery.

For the other ten unfriendlies who were called to testify, and became known as the Hollywood Ten,[39] HUAC was holding copies of their CPUSA membership cards. Finding the four obvious responses to the Communist question unsatisfactory, the Hollywood Ten sought to fashion their non-answer around the First Amendment:

> **First Amendment:** Congress shall make no law respecting an establishment of religion, or prohibiting the free exercise thereof; or abridging the freedom of speech, or of the press; or the right of the people peaceably to assemble, and to petition the Government for a redress of grievances.

The Hollywood Ten believed that freedom of speech and assembly permitted them to hold their own political beliefs beyond any interference or intrusion by the government. What if they cited the First Amendment as the basis for refusing to answer the Communist question? The strategy was risky.

Freedom of speech and the First Amendment are substantial subjects with a vast reach.[40] Speech such as fraud, perjury, slander, and the often-quoted "falsely shouting fire in a crowded theater" does not have blanket protection. At the time of the HUAC hearings, the Supreme Court, the ultimate arbiter of legality in such matters, had not yet considered the issue raised by the Hollywood Ten case. Two prior HUAC witnesses pursuing First Amendment defenses, Edward Barsky and Leon Josephson, were cited for contempt of Congress. Their prosecutions were still making their way through the courts. Among the considerations for the unfriendlies, and others such as Chandler who would pursue constitutional challenges over the next decade, was that the appeal process could take years. Moreover, they could end up in prison without the Supreme Court even reviewing their case.

Relying on advice from their lawyers, the Hollywood Ten decided to adopt a subtle element to their defense.[41] Rather than just passively refusing to answer on the basis of the First Amendment, they would take the offensive, insisting on responding in their own way and setting out on a long denouncement of the committee. If their filibuster were cut off prematurely by the impatient chair, in court they could have a contempt defense that they were not permitted to answer the question. In other words, they could both assert the First Amendment and fall back on a legal technicality.

The first unfriendly witness to be called by HUAC was screenwriter John Howard Lawson.[42] Lawson was widely regarded as the leader of the Hollywood CPUSA branch. His appearance would provide the template, both for the chair and witnesses, in the Hollywood Ten testimonies. It was contentious from the start. Lawson asked to read an opening statement, as some friendlies had been permitted to do. After reviewing the first sentence, Thomas ruled the statement out of order, provoking a protest of unfair treatment from Lawson.

Lawson did not wait for the Communist question to challenge the legitimacy of the committee. During the preliminaries, when asked about his associations with the Screen Writers Guild, Lawson claimed the inquiry was a violation of the Bill of Rights. When the Communist question was asked, Lawson launched into a condemnation of the hearing and HUAC, which was frequently interrupted by the Chair's furious gaveling and admonishments to be responsive. As the Ten's attorney anticipated, Thomas eventually directed officers to remove Lawson from the witness stand.

HUAC staff then presented evidence that Lawson was in the CPUSA, including a copy of his 1944 membership card. The scene of the intolerant Chair versus the belligerent witness followed by compelling evidence then seemed to be set on automatic repeat.[43] After the tenth iteration, and beyond the point of diminishing returns, HUAC abruptly pulled the plug on the hearings. The next witness would have been the sole actor on the unfriendly list, Larry Parks.[44]

The Hollywood Ten left Washington with the feeling that they had won the battle. To many observers though, the discordant hearing left a bad aftertaste with no admirable performances. Important reviews, legal and professional, awaited the Hollywood Ten.

Congress approved the HUAC recommendation of contempt citations. Indictments followed. With the prosecutors having the benefit of information obtained from illegal FBI wiretaps of the defense lawyer,[45] the Hollywood Ten were found guilty in Federal District Court. A three-judge panel of the Court of Appeals for the District of Columbia Circuit unanimously rejected their First Amendment defense.[46] The Court's opinion specifically stated that HUAC has "the *power*" (emphasis in original) to ask its witnesses the Communist question as well as "the power to effect punishment for failure or refusal to answer that question."

For the Supreme Court to review a case required certiorari, that is, approval from four of its members. In 1950, only Justices Hugo Black and William Douglas voted to take up the appeal of the Hollywood Ten. Prison sentences ranged from six months to a year. One curiosity is that the time in Danbury Federal Correctional Institute for writers Ring Lardner Jr. and Lester Cole overlapped with that of another principal from the hearing. Congressman Thomas was also in the Connecticut prison serving nine months after pleading the Fifth Amendment to a charge of salary fraud.[47]

For all its shortcomings, the hearings had revealed a CPUSA presence in Hollywood. The prosecutions during the Cold War were a threat to the wholesome image the film industry promoted of itself. On a track parallel to the court proceedings, the movie executives and their legal teams met to consider prophylactic measures. The meeting took place at the Waldorf Astoria Hotel in New York. The decision was made by the moguls to fire the Hollywood Ten and institute a blacklist for members of the CPUSA.[48] The outcome from their first collaboration was highly satisfactory to both Hoover and Thomas.

The plight of the Hollywood Ten played out in the environment of a country embarking on its second Red Scare. Since the 1946 midterm elections, President Truman had been on the defensive to demonstrate his anti-Communist bona fides. Early in 1947 he took two actions.[49] The first, in which he strongly believed, involved foreign aid. The other, motivated by political expediency, was domestic. What became known as the Truman Doctrine made financial support available to countries under threat of Communist takeover, such as Greece and Turkey. An executive order created a loyalty-security program supposedly to weed out Communists from federal employment positions.

Implementation of the loyalty-security program led, at the end of 1947, to Attorney General Tom Clark releasing a list of subversive organizations that included the CPUSA. While the list was intended as a tool to assist federal administrators in identifying disloyal employees, its usage went beyond the government and became widespread. Membership in these organizations, although still not explicitly a violation of law, could easily destroy a career in the public or private sector.

During the election year of 1948, the Truman Justice Department faced pressure from both the left and the right.[50] HUAC pressed Clark to proceed with Smith Act cases against CPUSA members.[51] The attorney general had another consideration. Following through against the CPUSA would leave the Democratic administration vulnerable to losing its more liberal supporters to the third-party challenge mounted by the Progressive Party's Henry Wallace. In July, Clark, relying on the voluminous files of the FBI, indicted the twelve-member National Board of the CPUSA for violations of the Smith Act. The trial shaped up as a test of the constitutionality and reach of the 1940 law.

Through a series of legal maneuvers, the CPUSA delayed the start of the trial for several months. During the interim, the case of the ailing William Z. Foster was separated from the others. The trial for the remaining eleven CPUSA leaders, *Dennis v. United States*, began in March 1949. As the prosecution had neither evidence that the defendants had advocated the forceful overthrow of the United States government nor that the CPUSA was plotting such an act, they set forth a two-part conspiracy argument. Underlying their case was a proviso that the Communist Party in the United States was reconstituted around 1935 and 1945, in both instances altering its policies on revolution and cooperation with capitalist systems. The government contended that the defendants had conspired to organize the CPUSA incarnation that had existed since 1945, a body which, in turn, included in its teachings the overthrow of the United States government by force.[52]

The trial proceedings lasted into October, punctuated by heated disputes between the judge and the defense team. After a day of deliberation, the jury reached a guilty verdict for each of the defendants. Sentences ranged from the three years for a combat veteran to five years for the others. Lawyers received time for contempt.

The CPUSA appealed the *Dennis* decision, citing innumerable grounds, among which was the contention that the Smith Act violated the First Amendment. In June 1950 a panel from the Second Circuit, including the respected jurist Learned Hand, heard the arguments. The three judges unanimously rejected every one of the CPUSA rationales.[53] In considering Freedom of Speech protection, an important consideration was the 1919 Oliver Wendell Holmes criterion of "whether the words used are of such a nature as to present a clear and present danger."[54] Subsequent Supreme Court rulings refined Holmes's test including the addition of a stipulation by Justice Louis Brandeis that the danger be "imminent."[55] For *Dennis*, Hand further modified the criterion and included it in a balancing formulation "ask[ing] whether the gravity of the 'evil,' discounted by its improbability, justifies such invasion of free speech as is necessary to avoid the danger." With an evil as consequential as government overthrow, Hand concluded that it trumped Freedom of Speech.

The final appeal was to the Supreme Court, which restricted their consideration to the constitutionality of the Smith Act. On a 6–2 vote in June 1951, the CPUSA leaders lost again.[56] Justice Tom Clark, the former attorney general who approved the original indictment, recused himself from the case. There were five separate opinions. Chief Justice Fred Vinson, in the majority and joined by three others, adopted the formulation of Hand. Hugo Black's dissent, excerpted below, made a powerful statement:

At the outset I want to emphasize what the crime involved in this case is, and what it is not. These petitioners were not charged with an attempt to overthrow the Government. They were not charged with overt acts of any kind designed to overthrow the Government. They were not even charged with saying anything or writing anything designed to overthrow the Government. The charge was that they agreed to assemble and to talk and publish certain ideas at a later date. The indictment is that they conspired to organize the Communist Party and to use speech or newspapers and other publications in the future to teach and advocate the forcible overthrow of the Government. No matter how it is worded, this is a virulent form of prior censorship of speech and press, which I believe the First Amendment forbids. I would hold Section 3 of the Smith Act authorizing this prior restraint unconstitutional on its face and as applied.

But let us assume, contrary to all constitutional ideas of fair criminal procedure, that petitioners although not indicted for the crime of actual advocacy, may be punished for it.... Undoubtedly, a governmental policy of unfettered communication of ideas does entail dangers. To the Founders of this Nation, however, the benefits derived from free expression were worth the risk....

Public opinion being what it now is, few will protest the conviction of these Communist petitioners. There is hope, however, that in calmer times, when present pressures, passions and fears subside, this or some later Court will restore the First Amendment liberties to the high preferred place where they belong in a free society.

The *Dennis* verdict and its affirmation meant that being a leader of the CPUSA officially constituted a crime. The government immediately went after the remaining leaders and the so-called second string. Over the next five years, more than one hundred CPUSA members were indicted, with most being convicted.[57] The Supreme Court declined to review any of the subsequent Smith Act cases until 1955, after the disgrace of Senator Joseph McCarthy. In a 1957 ruling, *Yates v. United States*,[58] the Court overturned convictions of some California second stringers on narrow grounds, leaving the Smith Act weakened, but still standing. Prosecutions under the law ended, but the damage was done.

The *Dennis* trial and its aftermath were devastating for the CPUSA. Operations moved deeper underground. With the considerable trial expenses and $80,000 in bail forfeiture from the four defendants who fled, the financial ramifications were enormous. Historian Ellen Schrecker described a new state of affairs in which the CPUSA found itself "virtually outlawed" while "the rest of the anticommunist crusade" was "legitimized."[59] In particular, the notion of First Amendment protection for CPUSA members was dealt another blow, and J. Edgar Hoover was emboldened.

Chandler and Natalie in 1951.
(COURTESY OF NATALIE ZEMON DAVIS)

CHAPTER FOUR

Scrutiny in Ann Arbor

In 1950 the Davises moved to Ann Arbor to embark on a new stage of their lives at the University of Michigan. Natalie continued her graduate study in early modern history. Chandler held the title instructor of mathematics. Despite beginning at the bottom of the faculty ladder, Chandler was positioned to launch his dream career, provided he could establish a successful research program.

The mathematics department at Michigan was strong, and, though not among the top few programs in the United States, was in the next tier. The topologist R. L. Wilder and analyst T. H. Hildebrandt were highly respected scholars and longtime Michigan professors. Hildebrandt was nearing the end of a lengthy tenure as chair, holding autocratic powers that were typical for the time. The department was ambitious, managing to attract some outstanding mathematicians for varying periods before they were called to more prestigious postings. For example, the eminent algebraist Richard Brauer arrived a couple of years prior to Chandler, and the rising-star topologist Raoul Bott one year after. Both Brauer and Bott were eventually lured away to Harvard where they remained until retirement.[1]

The Davises reached Ann Arbor as the second Red Scare was approaching its peak. During the previous year Mao Zedong gained control of China, and the Soviet Union successfully tested an atomic bomb. Then, early in 1950, came two dramatic revelations that alarmed many Americans. Physicist Klaus Fuchs confessed to spying on the Manhattan Project for the Soviet Union and Senator Joseph McCarthy spoke in Wheeling, West Virginia, alleging the infiltration of CPUSA members into the State Department (giving rise to the "ism" that carries his name). With the beginning of the Korean War in the summer of 1950, many Americans viewed communism as an existential threat. HUAC was redoubling its efforts to expose anyone with ties to the evaporating movement.

Chandler transferred to an Ann Arbor branch of the CPUSA. The risks of detection by the FBI and the Michigan State Police called for a high level of secrecy among members. Some idea of the extent of these measures is provided by the following story: Steve Smale was a mathematics student at Michigan who joined another CPUSA branch about this time.[2] Although Chandler and Smale began a long-term friendship through their shared scholarly and political interests, neither was aware of the other's CPUSA membership until decades later. Even so, the concealment was under attack by determined counterintelligence foes in the government.

The CPUSA presence in Ann Arbor was modest. Liberal and conservative viewpoints were more abundant. In the mathematics department, Wilder and Hildebrandt were, respectively, exemplars of these ideologies. The liberal Council of Arts, Sciences, and Professions was a local organization, of mostly faculty and graduate students, in which both Chandler and Natalie became active. Not long after, the Council selected Chandler to serve as their Treasurer. In earning this position Chandler was executing the CPUSA practice of gaining influence in organizations that could advance Party objectives. The FBI and HUAC regarded the Ann Arbor

Council of Arts, Sciences, and Professions as a "Communist front group."[3]

HUAC's announcement of February 1952 hearings in Detroit, ostensibly to investigate Communist infiltration of the defense industry, activated the left wing at the University of Michigan. Rumors began to circulate of the committee making a follow-up visit to out Communists in Ann Arbor. Naturally, the possibility of these hearings was of considerable interest to the Council of Arts, Sciences, and Professions.

Natalie's reaction to the prospective HUAC visit was that of a scholar. She proceeded to the library where she pored over HUAC's publications as well as newspaper accounts and commentaries on its hearings.[4] Then, in collaboration with a young psychology lecturer, Elizabeth Douvan, Natalie drafted a critical essay about the committee. A sense of their perspective is given by its section titles including "A Decade of 'Smear' Tactics," "What Are 'Un-American' Ideas," "Who Has Been Attacked by the Committee?," "The Committee's Contribution to American Life: Thought Purge and Inquisition," and "Here Is What You Can Do to Prevent Thought Control in America." The Council of Arts, Sciences, and Professions reviewed the piece, and authorized its distribution under their auspices. As an officer of the organization, Chandler arranged for the printing and layout in an authorless twelve-page pamphlet titled *Operation Mind*.[5]

A worker at the print shop found the message of *Operation Mind* alarming. Her husband took the initiative to provide a copy of the pamphlet to the FBI, along with the name of the individual, H. Chandler Davis, who had ordered its reproduction.[6] This information was subsequently conveyed by the FBI to HUAC.[7] HUAC was particularly sensitive to the publicity it received. When Chandler later appeared before a HUAC subcommittee, a substantial portion of the questioning involved *Operation Mind*.

The 1952 HUAC visit to Ann Arbor never materialized. In

the spring, Natalie traveled to Lyon, France, to pursue archival research for her thesis. Chandler remained in Michigan until joining her over the summer. During this period, he got caught up in some fallout from the Detroit hearing. While this incident is largely peripheral to our main HUAC story, it does illuminate the contemporary Ann Arbor political environment and Chandler's involvement in it.[8]

The controversy began when Arthur McPhaul, who had appeared under subpoena before HUAC in Detroit, was invited by the university's Young Progressives to speak on campus. McPhaul was the executive secretary of the Michigan chapter of the Civil Rights Congress, an organization on the Attorney General's list of subversive organizations. At the HUAC hearing, McPhaul had asserted his Fifth Amendment rights in declining to answer the Communist question as well as to produce records pertaining to the Civil Rights Congress.

A University of Michigan policy, aimed at shielding students from any "advocacy of the subversion of the government of the United States,"[9] required campus organizations to obtain advance approval for their speakers from the University Lecture Committee. Over the past fifteen years only three applications had been turned down, each for a self-avowed Communist. The Lecture Committee provisionally rejected the Young Progressives' request for McPhaul as well as for Abner Greene, neither of whom had admitted to CPUSA membership, requiring proof that the speeches would not be subversive. Greene, also an officer of an organization on the Attorney General's list, had just completed a jail sentence for contempt. His offense was refusing to cooperate with the government in locating the CPUSA leaders who jumped bail following their convictions under the Smith Act.

The handling by the Lecture Committee of the McPhaul and Greene cases generated considerable controversy on campus. On its front page, the student newspaper, the *Michigan Daily*, editorially condemned the *raison d' être* and actions of the Lecture

Committee, stating: "They showed tendencies even more deplorable than the actual rule which they must enforce. They were willing to require proof of innocence, rather than guilt."[10]

A few days later, the *Daily* covered a speech delivered by McPhaul at a private dinner for about twenty people in the Student Union. The article described the event as taking place "under mysterious sponsorship."[11] The newspaper's investigation revealed that the arrangements for the affair had been made by a person identifying himself as Henry Gerard, an apparent pseudonym. The speech had not been approved by the University Lecture Committee.

Over the next two months, the administration authorized a series of investigations into whether the clandestine McPhaul dinner involved violations of university regulations. Steve Smale was among the students who were interrogated about their participation. While Smale had in fact attended the gathering, he refused to cooperate with the investigation. In the end, no punishment was administered to students for taking part in the dinner. Smale and four others were placed on probation and forced to resign from offices in extracurricular activities for their lack of cooperation with university authorities.

Meanwhile, a student-wide referendum called for the abolition of the Lecture Committee. This sentiment failed to sway the committee. Additional proposed speakers, with alleged subversive connections, were held up or barred. Chandler, who strongly supported the students, campaigned to lift the restriction on controversial campus speakers. His letter to the editor in the May 10 *Daily* announced a resolution of the Council of Arts, Sciences, and Professions urging clearance of the McPhaul case students and elimination of the University Lecture Committee.

Cognizant of the limited influence of the "small band of do-gooders" on the liberal Council, Chandler went further.[12] Hayward Keniston, the outgoing Dean of the College of Literature, Science, & the Arts, had supported the student referendum against the Lecture Committee. In an unusual move for a second-year instructor, Chandler reached out to the dean to find an avenue for the faculty to take a stand on the issue. The outcome was their Davis-Keniston collaboration on a petition drive in which seventy-five members of the faculty called for a special meeting to consider a position of the college on the lecture policy. The faculty approved a resolution that student organizations be provided with the authority to select their own speakers.[13] As with that of the students, the faculty statement had no discernible effect on administrative policy. Nevertheless, Chandler had taken a risk in leading an initiative that, although apparently unnoticed,[14] would have been of considerable interest to the FBI and HUAC.

This is not to say that the FBI was unaware of Chandler's political activities in Ann Arbor. One of his friends, from the Council of Arts, Sciences, and Professions, was providing the FBI with regular reports. The informant was Irving Rozian, a local engineer who lectured at the university.[15] His May update with the Davises' 1952 European travel plans included other intelligence. Rozian described his own recent recruitment by Chandler into an Ann Arbor branch of the CPUSA. The Detroit FBI office immediately relayed the information to Director Hoover in a memorandum that included a preposterous implication about sinister undercover work. "The informant also advised that he gathers from DAVIS that the latter is one of maybe four or five mathematicians doing advanced work in Quantum Mechanics Theory . . . (N.B. It is believed this theory is one of the basic mathematical theories upon which nuclear and atomic energy theories are based.)"[16]

As with his application for an Atomic Energy Commission fellowship, the covertly obtained information linking a CPUSA member to atomic energy research prompted further action at FBI headquarters. Memoranda about the subversive Davises and their travel were sent by special messenger from Director Hoover to the heads of security at the Atomic Energy

Commission and the Department of State.[17] As we shall see, the State Department, at least, would take action.

Since he was to be in France for the entire summer of 1952, Chandler took a leave of absence from the CPUSA. In Lyon, he found Natalie at work in an archive uncovering materials on the lives of the town's sixteenth-century artisans. These records would launch her groundbreaking thesis that, when completed seven years later, would be titled *Protestantism and the Printing Workers of Lyon: A Study in Religion and Social Class.* Her focus on the working class departed from the traditional historical lens on the Reformation, which concentrated mainly on the lives of theologians and the privileged.

The summer in France was a significant interlude for the Davises, concluding with Natalie's first pregnancy. Not only had Natalie found an innovative research direction, but away from the doctrinaire CPUSA pressures for Marxist purity the couple bonded with a heterogeneous assortment of leftist students. The experience reminded Chandler of his days at Harvard prior to joining the CPUSA.[18]

Chandler returned to Ann Arbor in the fall and reinstated his Party membership. In November, two strangers appeared at the Davis apartment door. They were representatives of the State Department who, without providing any reason, confiscated their passports. For Natalie, the loss of the prospect for follow-up archival work in Europe was a devastating blow. It would take her years to find a partial workaround.

Over time, the Davises came to attribute the State Department's revocation of their passports to the FBI's association of Chandler with *Operation Mind*.[19] An examination of Chandler's FBI files in 2020 shows that the FBI, unlike HUAC, demonstrated little interest in *Operation Mind*. A chain of evidence in the files indicates that the May 1952 report from the informant and Hoover's notification to the State Department were what triggered the confiscation.[20]

Out of a life immersed in CPUSA culture, Chandler was all too familiar with stories of family friends being fired or served with subpoenas. He had already given up a prestigious fellowship and good job to avoid compromising positions. And while exposure was a danger to which he had long been reconciled, the passport confiscation confirmed that he was under scrutiny, even if he had no idea that an engineer friend was the informant.[21]

At the same time, several factors caused Chandler to have serious misgivings about remaining in the CPUSA. What follows are excerpts from a 2019 email thread where he and I discussed the evolution of his feelings during the 1952–1953 period.

Chandler wrote:

> During my years in the Party, I was more apt than most to be dubious about the Party line, and I was much more open than most to respectful political cooperation with non-Party people including Trotskyites. . . .
>
> I had concerns since 1952 about the CPUSA supporting so unwaveringly the Soviet government which was harsh on dissidents. (I didn't perceive HOW harsh until several years later.) . . .
>
> In 1952 I had very helpful conversations with my friend and Math Dept colleague Ed Moïse. He pointed out, putting documentation before me which I had no reason to challenge, that the Soviet government had killed or driven out of the country a strikingly large portion of its initial leadership, and I agreed with him that whatever else they accomplished they plainly ruled by terror. . . .
>
> I was willing for the sake of belonging to a powerful movement to stay in the Party and maintain a critical stance within it, as my father did. What had changed between 1952 and 1953 is that my Party membership had become totally useless to my actual political agitation, which was done through organizations like ASP, student groups, etc. The CP had simply become a drag . . . it was out of steam.

Following up, I wrote:

The question is sometimes asked how smart people such as yourself could have held their views for so long despite what had gone on in the Soviet Union. It seems to me that you were experiencing Communism in theory and seeing capitalism in action. Both had serious problems, but you were seeing the effects in the United States on Blacks and labor, giving good reason to mistrust capitalist portrayals of what was happening in the Soviet Union. Is this too simplistic?

To which Chandler replied:

Well, by 1953 Natalie & I were frightened by the repression & brutality we saw in the Soviet Union. We didn't like that, and we didn't have any clear idea of how we would accommodate to it if we lived there, but (1) we didn't have any plan to live there so this wasn't urgent, and (2) as I mentioned to you before (message of 30 March, last para), I didn't believe there were anywhere near so MANY in gulag or murdered as alleged. . . . The thing I think I was awfully slow to see is that you can't claim to have a worker's state if the workers are scared shitless of the secret police. I like to emphasize this insight by recalling the Museum of the Revolution in Red Square: one of the many fascinating photos on the wall from those days was a genuine mass demonstration, with banners "Vsyu vlast' sovetam": all power to the soviets—but the visitor is not told what those who know the history recall, that less than six months after that demo Lenin had the workers' soviets smashed. In other words, as I said (message of 31 March), I was slow to see how very early the promise of socialism had been defeated, not by the Whites or by Stalin or by Trotsky, though they all contributed to the disaster, but by Lenin.

Chandler recalled that his father, Horace, was critical of CPUSA leaders who visited the Soviet Union and returned with less than candid reports of the conditions there. Natalie, who was cced in the discussion, added:

During my few years when I was in touch with people in or close to the CP (along with many other friends of different democratic or progressive views), I was not focused on the Soviet Union and did **not** take it as a model for the future I was hoping for. I was interested in the promise of SOCIALISM in America, and was also very concerned to fight racial prejudice, repression of free speech, anti-Semitism, and continuing support for the Nazis (remember the date). I did not think much about the Soviet Union except when matters of foreign policy came up—and I wanted very much to work against the possibility of war and the dangers of an atomic bomb.

Reformisy

For Chandler, his 1953 desire to leave the CPUSA was complicated by the problem of how exactly to make an amicable exit. He was not in any way renouncing his past activity. It was important to him that his withdrawal not be construed as "slamming the door on CP." Rather, he would be "only let[ting] that part of his political life drop."[22] Chandler wanted "old friends who continued as loyal CPers to remain personal friends. . . . Not to mention the still more numerous old comrades of whom I d[id]n't know whether they were in the Party or not."

No form existed for resignation from the CPUSA and of course there was no website with a link on which to click for terminating membership. Many people left by simply drifting away, scaling their participation down to nothing.[23] As would be pointed out by skeptical HUAC members at hearings, the resignation by inactivity approach provided no proof of separation.

For the summer of 1953 the Davises, including their infant son Aaron, traveled to Chandler's parents' summer home in Sandwich, Massachusetts. Once again, Chandler took a leave of absence from the CPUSA. His method of leaving the Party was that he "simply didn't get back in touch" upon his return.[24] While Chandler considered himself to have left the CPUSA, there was then a period where he could presumably change his mind and still be welcomed back. That he was really out of the Party would be established by his follow-up to a second visit from uninvited government representatives, this time to his office, on November 10. Chandler narrates:

> So clearly there was a touch of "here we go again" in autumn 1953 when two unprofessorial types showed up in 374 West Engineering Building and said they were from the House Committee on Un-American Activities. "Congratulations," I gibed. They said they wanted to talk to me, but this was altogether perfunctory, quite unlike the protracted interviews I know they had with others. In short order they had served me with a subpoena and departed.[25]

In a memo to his superior, one of the HUAC visitors, investigator Donald Appell, gave this description of Chandler's response: "He refused, when advised that the Committee had evidence with respect to his Communist Party affiliations, to discuss the subject. As a matter of fact, he ordered me from his office."[26]

It had been six years since the Hollywood Ten received their subpoenas to testify before the committee. Subsequent cases had provided some clarifications to the legal ramifications of relying on the First and Fifth Amendments. Suffice it to say that neither of these defenses, which will be discussed in the next chapter, guaranteed much protection. Chandler would consult widely in deciding on his course of action. What is significant to note for now is that, unlike with his handling of the Atomic Energy Commission Fellowship, he did not inform the CPUSA of his subpoena. Having purposely not followed this expectation for a member confirms that Chandler, by his own (in)action, was no longer in the CPUSA, from their perspective or his.

On the day following his visit to Chandler, Appell delivered subpoenas and sought to interview two other Michigan faculty, assistant professor of zoology Clement Markert and associate professor of mathematics Nate Coburn. Markert told Appell that he would seek legal advice before deciding on how to respond to questions from HUAC.[27] He did indicate, however, an openness to discuss his own background, but a refusal to talk about others. Coburn, who had been diagnosed with multiple sclerosis, also declined to discuss his affiliations with Appell, citing his physician's admonition for maintaining tranquility.[28]

More substantive interviews took place with Mark Nickerson and Lawrence Klein, respectively, associate professor of pharmacology and lecturer of economics. HUAC had information, through informants, that both Nickerson and Klein were CPUSA members in the 1940s. Nickerson admitted to Appell his association with an allegedly subversive organization, but he frustrated the investigator by denying CPUSA membership and asserting that he would refuse to answer the Communist question before the committee. Appell's memo on Nickerson included the information that, on the next day, Nickerson informed the university of his prior CPUSA membership.[29]

In contrast, Klein, who had already disclosed his CPUSA past to the university, was forthright with the HUAC investigators about his background. He confessed to belonging to the Party in Chicago for about a year during the period 1946–47, as well as to teaching courses in Communist-affiliated programs. Notes on the interview revealed the investigator's skepticism over Klein's inability to recall more than one full name from his associations.[30]

Klein was early into a remarkable career that would include the 1980 Nobel Prize in Economics at the age of sixty. Born in Nebraska, he received his PhD in 1944 under Paul Samuelson at MIT, after just two years of graduate study. He then held a variety of postdoctoral research positions, bringing him to the Institute for Social Research at the University of Michigan in 1949. The following year, the Michigan economics department recruited Klein to teach a graduate sequence in his specialty, econometrics, adding the title of lecturer to his research associateship. It quickly became clear that Klein was a powerful scholar who was a leader in the shaping of his rapidly emerging field. Members of the department saw that a permanent association with him was a special opportunity for the university.[31]

During the academic year 1952–53, discussions took place in the economics department over appointing Klein to a professorship, the rank commensurate with his accomplishments yet an unheard-of advancement from the level of lecturer. In the midst of the promotion consideration, Klein voluntarily disclosed his CPUSA background, leading to a suspension of the discussions. While the revelations were troubling to both the university and HUAC, his willingness to come forward placed Klein in a different class from the other faculty who were subpoenaed by the committee.

HUAC's original list of University of Michigan "subversives" included additional names. When Michigan president Harlan Hatcher learned, in early 1953, of the possibility of a HUAC visit, he reached out to the committee to express his willingness to cooperate.[32] Prior to the issuance of any subpoenas, Hatcher was informed that fifteen campus subversives had been identified for testimony.[33] Hoping to reduce the number, Hatcher dispatched Michigan vice president Marvin Niehuss to Washington.[34] Niehuss met with HUAC staff to review the files. Among the suspects was a faculty member for whom their corroboration was merely a picture of him attending a speech by a known Communist. Another professor had been invited to speak by the Committee for Soviet-American Friendship, an alleged Communist front. Arguing that the evidence was too thin, Niehuss succeeded in having these faculty and others deleted from the list of potential witnesses. Two graduate students in economics, Myron Sharpe and Ed Shaffer, were later subpoenaed and would testify at the hearing for Davis, Markert, Coburn, and Nickerson.

Publicity photograph of Larry Parks, 1950.
(COLUMBIA PICTURES)

CHAPTER FIVE

Deciding on a Response to HUAC

HUAC subpoenas directed Davis, Coburn, Markert, and Nickerson to appear in Lansing on January 18, 1954. The hearing, which was postponed several times, finally took place on May 10 before a subcommittee chaired by Michigan Republican Kit Clardy. By this time, most current and former CPUSA members who declined to answer the Communist question were asserting their right under the Fifth Amendment against "be[ing] compelled in any criminal case to be a witness against himself." Early on, HUAC had challenged the legitimacy of such claims with contempt citations.

The legal basis for HUAC witnesses using the Fifth Amendment became grounded in the 1950 Supreme Court case *Blau v. United States* pertaining to grand jury interrogation on Communist matters.[1] The Court ruled that witnesses could broadly use the privilege to avoid answering questions concerning their knowledge of and association with the CPUSA. In his opinion for the Court, Hugo Black wrote: "Whether such admissions by themselves would support a conviction under a criminal statute is immaterial. Answers to the questions asked by the grand jury would have furnished a link in the chain of evidence needed in a prosecution of petitioner for violation of (or conspiracy to violate) the Smith Act." Based on the comparable nature of grand jury and congressional investigations, most HUAC contempt charges for usage of the Fifth Amendment were subsequently dismissed.[2]

HUAC and its witnesses went on to adjust their strategies. In 1951 the committee again targeted Hollywood where the Communist blacklist remained in effect. Actor Larry Parks, who was on deck and eluded the Hollywood Ten's fate when their hearing adjourned, was called to testify. The former CPUSA member knew that the Fifth Amendment approach, though sparing him from prison, would destroy his career. Parks voluntarily admitted to his past Communist activity. He was shaken to find that his confession was insufficient for the committee. Parks was asked to provide the names of other CPUSA members. Moreover, since he had voluntarily responded to the Communist question, under the so-called *waiver doctrine* from the recent *Rogers v. United States*[3] decision in a grand jury case, he had waived his right to use the Fifth Amendment.[4]

Trapped, Parks implored: "Don't present me with the choice of either being in contempt of this committee and going to jail or forcing me to crawl through the mud to be an informer." Later that day, in executive session, a broken Parks disclosed a dozen names.[5] When his testimony became known, the waiver doctrine lesson was clear to anyone who had ever been associated with the CPUSA. To avoid naming names without being subject to contempt, all substantive questions required a Fifth Amendment response. In Hollywood, the Fifth Amendment credit was the end to employment in the motion picture industry.

Naming names had its own downside. In addition to the guilty feelings of betrayal, the enmity of old friends, and being identified by loathsome epithets, career damage was not necessarily averted. For example, Larry Parks was dropped from his next movie by Columbia Pictures.[6] He would never recover, professionally or personally.

In his book about blacklisted screenwriter Carl Foreman, Glenn Frankel described what was required to salvage a film career from a HUAC hearing: "But acquiescence alone was also not sufficient. To achieve redemption, witnesses were required to go through a three-step process: acknowledge their prior left-wing activities with deep regret, praise the committee for its important and heroic work, and demonstrate the credibility of their transformation from Red to red-blooded American by disclosing the names of other subversives."[7]

After Parks, all Red-tainted witnesses faced the unpalatable choice between "taking the Fifth" and "naming names," if they wanted a safe harbor from criminal prosecution. The pressure on them was enormous, usually exacerbated by family considerations. Outside the motion picture industry, the consequences were at times less systematic, but typically the Fifth was followed by job termination and considerable difficulty on the employment market.[8]

A few witnesses, who could not abide either naming names or the Fifth, tried other routes, receiving contempt indictments that they contested through litigation. One approach, known as the "diminished Fifth," was to admit to a CPUSA background and refuse to implicate others, not invoking the Fifth Amendment. Although never gaining approval by a court ruling per se, this risky strategy usually succeeded on narrow grounds via various technicalities.[9] The diminished Fifth was of little use in Hollywood where non-cooperation assured blacklisting, but some people in other occupations held on to their jobs and some dignity while battling the government in the courts.

Republicans regained control of the House in the 1952 election after four years in the minority. Harold Velde from Illinois became the chair of HUAC. He was a former FBI agent who had been elected to Congress behind the slogan:

"Get the Reds out of Washington and Washington out of the Red."[10]

Velde set the HUAC sights on exposing college faculty with Communist backgrounds. FBI files and the name-generating nature of the process supplied many targets. In 1953 over one hundred college teachers received HUAC subpoenas.[11] To manage the volume of traffic, Velde delegated the questioning to regional subcommittees.

Institutions of higher learning, in turn, faced the problems of what to do about faculty who were called before the committee and the negative publicity from their hearings. Early in 1953, the Association of American Universities (AAU), a prestigious organization of thirty-seven leading universities, weighed in with some high-profile guidance. The AAU statement included the assertion that "a scholar must have integrity and independence. This renders impossible adherence to such a regime as Russia and its satellites. No person who accepts or advocates such principles and methods has any place in a university . . . present membership in the Communist Party . . . extinguishes the right to a university position." The Association advised further that "invocation of the Fifth Amendment places upon a professor a heavy burden of proof of his fitness to hold a teaching position and lays upon his university an obligation to re-examine his qualifications for membership in its society."[12]

In effect, the AAU was urging professors to name names. Most faculty who did so chose this course reluctantly. These professors often set out to disclose as few names as possible, or those of people who were already known to the committee (small consolation to the renamed). A difficulty with this strategy was the uncertainty of knowing how aggressively their interrogators might pursue additional information. After all, enlarging their suspect pool was a priority for HUAC. Providing the committee with a meager list could provoke demands for more names, at a point where there was no turning back. Having committed

Names

to naming names, an effective tactic was to assuage the mood of the narcissistic committee with injections of contrition and flattery as mentioned by Frankel for Hollywood witnesses seeking redemption.

MIT mathematician Norman Levinson admitted to his earlier CPUSA membership before a HUAC subcommittee in Washington on April 23, 1953. He ingratiated himself with the congressmen by offering the view that (current CPUSA members were in need of psychiatric care.) Levinson managed to escape without revealing any new names. He repeated from the list supplied on the previous day by his branch comrade W. T. Martin, and confirmed others already known from prior testimony. One week later the MIT Executive Committee approved continuance of Levinson and Martin in the mathematics department, without penalty and in "good standing."[13]

For faculty taking the Fifth, unlike the MIT mathematicians, disciplinary action could be expected. The main question was whether they would be fired. Untenured faculty were typically terminated, either immediately or at the end of their contracts. Those with tenure were by no means safe, but some escaped with a reprimand or probation. The nature of their follow-up reviews varied from institution to institution.[14] University by-laws, typically written before the second Red Scare, did not specify sanctions for CPUSA activity. At the University of Michigan, President Harlan Hatcher attempted to set the statutory ground by submitting the AAU statement to the faculty for ratification.[15] Rather than an endorsement, the University of Michigan Senate approved an alternative to the procedure for dismissal that provided an expedited review process for "exceptional cases which threaten direct and immediate injury to the public reputation or the essential functions of the University."

Clement Markert and Mark Nickerson were both willing to testify forthrightly before HUAC about their CPUSA memberships, which had ended by the time of their joining the Michigan faculty. The thought of naming names, however, was repugnant to both professors. They decided to take the Fifth and hope to save their jobs in the subsequent university review where their excellent scholarly records might be expected to carry greater weight than obtaining names of Communists.

Having already revealed his past CPUSA connections to HUAC and the university, Lawrence Klein, not surprisingly, decided to cooperate in the hearing. In return, he was given the benefit of testifying in a secret executive session rather than face the public interrogation awaiting Markert and Nickerson. Nate Coburn continued his course of seeking to be excused from testimony because of his health issues. The graduate students Myron Sharpe and Ed Shaffer would take the Fifth, possibly under direction from the CPUSA.

This left Chandler, at age twenty-seven and with twenty months remaining on his instructor's contract, the youngest and the least secure professionally of the faculty.[16] Coburn and Nickerson were tenured associate professors. Between the receipt of his subpoena and testimony at the HUAC hearing, Markert was recommended for promotion from assistant professor to associate professor by both his department and college.[17] The process was stopped days before the hearing when Markert informed the administration of his upcoming testimony. Thus, while Markert had passed muster for tenure, Davis was merely approaching consideration for advancement to the untenured rank of assistant professor.

For Chandler, a subpoena had been more a matter of *when* than *if*.[18] His thinking about how to deal with the likely eventuality intensified over the prior summer with his father's testimony in Chicago before the Senate Internal Security Subcommittee (SISS) on June 9, 1953. SISS was a Senate committee established a few years earlier that was proceeding in a fashion similar to HUAC. At the time of his SISS appearance, Horace was a tenured associate professor of economics at the University of Kansas City. In his testimony, Davis protested that the committee was "operating to establish a conformity of opinion" in violation of the First Amendment. When asked a variant of the Communist question, he declined to answer, maintaining his rights under both the First and Fifth Amendments.[19]

SISS, noting his invocation of the Fifth Amendment, did not cite Horace for contempt. So, when Chandler received his subpoena in November, his father was facing formal charges for dismissal from the University of Kansas City. Horace was fired in December, following a recommendation from a committee consisting of administrators, faculty, and trustees. Horace unsuccessfully challenged his termination in federal court.[20] A major takeaway for Chandler was that, despite his father's and others' principled assertions of the First Amendment before SISS and HUAC, in the press they were marginalized as *Fifth Amendment Communists*.[21]

Chandler drew the conclusion that a First Amendment argument, if it was to gain traction, necessitated eschewal of the Fifth Amendment. But if he did this, he would almost certainly face dismissal and a contempt of Congress indictment. The upside to Chandler was that through his prosecution he would gain standing to challenge the constitutionality of the hearings in the courts. While the contention that the HUAC hearings infringed on freedom of speech had already failed for the Hollywood Ten, the matter had never made it to the Supreme Court. Chandler was fully aware that relying on the First Amendment to reach the highest court and obtain a favorable ruling was a high-risk venture with only a small chance of success. Yet the possibility of ending the persecution of Americans for left-wing political beliefs was of great importance to him. In selecting this route, he had the full support of Natalie, who independently had come to advocate the same strategy.[22]

Notwithstanding its past defeat in the courts, Chandler's course had received some judicial support. There were two separate Court of Appeals dissents with arguments that compelling citizens to disclose their political beliefs and associations to a congressional committee was inconsistent with the First Amendment. This principle has been characterized as the freedom *not* to speak.[23] As stated earlier, the Hollywood Ten lost their First Amendment challenge in the Court of Appeals for the District of Columbia Circuit on a 3–0 vote in 1949, and the Supreme Court denied certiorari.

In the Hollywood Ten decision, *Lawson v. United States*,[24] Judge Bennett Champ Clark's opinion for the Court of Appeals reaffirmed the reasoning of the two-judge majority, of which he had been a member, in the *Barsky v. United States* case. Edward Barsky was the chairman of the Joint Anti-Fascist Refugee Committee, an organization that HUAC regarded as a CPUSA front. At a 1946 HUAC hearing, Barsky refused to surrender the records of his organization. He was cited for contempt and then convicted in federal court. The subsequent affirmation in the Court of Appeals for the District of Columbia Circuit[25] included a strong dissent from Judge Henry Edgerton that contained this statement about HUAC's tactics and its chilling effect on free speech:

> The investigation restricts freedom of speech by uncovering and stigmatizing expressions of unpopular views. The Committee gives wide publicity to its proceedings. This exposes the men and women whose views are advertised to risks of insult, ostracism, and lasting loss of employment. Persons disposed to express unpopular views privately or to a selected group are often not disposed to risk the consequences to themselves and their families that publication may entail. The Committee's practice of advertising and stigmatizing unpopular views is therefore a strong deterrent to any expression, however private, of such views.
>
> The investigation also restricts freedom of speech by forcing people to express views. Freedom of speech is freedom in respect to speech and includes freedom not to speak.

Judge Edgerton's dissent identified other defects in the conviction of Barsky, among them the reliance of the HUAC enabling act on vague terms such as "un-American" and "subversive." The Court of Appeals majority found these words to convey a "clear meaning" when viewed in their context. Additionally, the Barsky Court's opinion, on which the Hollywood Ten decision relied, asserted that Communism "is antithetical to the principles which underlie" the United States government and "is a potential menace" to it. Then followed a balancing argument between the needs of a HUAC inquiry into Communism and freedom of speech:

> The problem is the relative necessity of the public interest as against the private rights. . . . That the protection of private rights upon occasion involves an invasion of those rights is in theory a paradox but, in the world as it happens to be, is a realistic problem requiring a practical answer. That invasion should never occur except upon necessity, but unless democratic government (by which we mean government premised upon individual human rights) can protect itself by means commensurate with danger, it is doomed.

The Hollywood Ten appeals court unanimously reaffirmed Barsky, quoting liberally from the majority opinion. *Lawson* unambiguously upheld the authority of HUAC for responsiveness of its witnesses to the Communist question. Just before Barsky, the Court of Appeals for the Second Circuit reached the same 2–1 outcome in affirming the conviction in *United States v. Josephson*.[26]

Leon Josephson was a lawyer who was suspected by HUAC of subversive activities. At a HUAC subcommittee hearing, he refused to be sworn in for testimony. Following his conviction, Josephson appealed on the basis of several matters including the constitutionality of the law authorizing HUAC investigations. The majority quoted from a federal report that found Communists and fascists to be "[t]he most immediate threat to the right to freedom of opinion and expression." They ruled:

> The power of Congress to gather facts of the most intense public concern, such as these, is not diminished by the unchallenged right of individuals to speak their minds within lawful limits. When speech, or propaganda, or whatever it at the moment be called, clearly presents an immediate danger to national security, the protection of the First Amendment ceases.

The Josephson Court of Appeals dissent was by Judge Charles Clark, who, like Edgerton, sharply criticized HUAC for its tactics as well as its manipulation of the terms "un-American" and "subversive." Clark framed the constitutional issue in terms of limits on the congressional power of investigation. Clark contended that HUAC was exploiting the vagueness of its charge to abuse its authority, in violation of the First Amendment. As with Edgerton, Clark lamented the effect of the HUAC investigations, going even further to imply that it was un-American:

> All of this points to and underlines the real vice of so vague and ambiguous an authority when so determinedly marshalled against minority views. It invites and justifies an attempt to enforce conformity of political thinking, to penalize the new and the original, to label as subversive or un-American the attempt to devise new approaches for the public welfare, in short to damn that very kind of initiative in experimentation which has made our democracy grow and flourish.

The 1948 civil libertarian dissents of Judges Edgerton and Charles Clark left the possibility that Chandler's strategy was not quite as far-fetched as indicated by the better-known unequivocal ruling of the Court of Appeals against the Hollywood Ten. In particular, two votes in his favor on a panel from a different circuit might even induce the Supreme Court to review the then conflicting decisions. Compounding the uncertainty, of what was undoubtedly a long shot, were the intensification of the second Red Scare and the ever-changing personnel on the federal bench. Between the Hollywood Ten hearings and the subsequent certiorari consideration by the Supreme Court, liberal Justices Frank Murphy and Wiley Rutledge died and were replaced by the more conservatively ruling Tom Clark and Sherman Minton.[27]

Having decided on his response to HUAC, Chandler met with Hatcher to inform him of what to expect at the hearing. The conversation was cordial, but their priorities were starkly different. Hatcher was concerned about the adverse impact on the university from the publicity of faculty associated with the CPUSA. He advised Chandler, for whom naming names was a nonstarter, to follow the AAU course of cooperation with HUAC. Of the Michigan faculty testifying before HUAC, only Klein would adhere to Hatcher's guidance.

Chandler was not alone in relying exclusively on the First Amendment to challenge the HUAC hearings. A few others, outside Michigan, opted for the same perilous and principled approach. Chandler, however, was probably unique in a subtle distinction of attitude. For him acquittal on a technicality would be a disappointment, if the Supreme Court did not put an end to HUAC's practices. Chandler's objective made the selection of legal counsel especially important.

HUAC permitted its witnesses to be accompanied by attorneys, not to perform a legal defense such as cross-examinations, but rather to provide advice to their clients. Chandler hoped to secure a skilled lawyer, one who appreciated his strategic view, to sit with him at the hearing and press the case through the courts. At the height of the second Red Scare, many in the legal profession were deterred by the guilt by association that could follow representing an unfriendly HUAC witness.[28] Only a small number of attorneys were willing to take on the risk. Through his left-wing connections in Ann Arbor, Chandler had become acquainted with a spirited, young lawyer, Ann Fagan Ginger, whom he believed suited his needs.

Ann Fagan was born in East Lansing, Michigan.[29] She received undergraduate and law degrees at the University of Michigan in the 1940s. Her endeavor to be a labor lawyer was hampered by gender discrimination and her past radical activity. In 1952, she moved to Boston with her husband, Ray Ginger, who had taken a position in the Harvard Business School.

Following his subpoena, Chandler asked Ann Fagan Ginger to represent him. To his dismay Ginger declined, citing possible conflicts between court schedules and her parental responsibilities with two infant children. She did, however, inform Chandler of the scholarly view on freedom of speech advocated by philosopher Alexander Meiklejohn. This would provide Chandler with an innovative constitutional basis that he embraced for his court challenge.

Here we will focus on the aspects of the philosophy that pertain to Chandler's contention that the HUAC investigations were unconstitutional. The starting point for Meiklejohn[30] is that under the Constitution, the United States is a self-governing nation in which the People, its sovereigns, delegate specific powers to the legislative, executive, and judicial branches. The jurisdiction of each branch is restricted by its respective article with ultimate authority resting with the People who elect the Congress and president, who in turn determine the judges.

To understand Meiklejohn's perspective on the First Amendment, it is helpful to break the core of its statement into the two parts: "Congress shall make no law . . . abridging" and "freedom of speech." Of particular importance is the unqualified nature of the first part and its uniqueness as such among the Ten Amendments. These elements in the carefully constructed document can only be interpreted to mean an absolute proscription on Congress at all times regarding restrictions on freedom of speech. As to the second part, Meiklejohn distinguishes "freedom of speech" from "speech." According to Meiklejohn, the First Amendment pertains to speech that bears upon matters of the public interest, the scope of which is enumerated in the preamble to the Constitution.

After rebelling against repressive colonial rule, the Founding Fathers determined that in their new form of governing, the People must possess this freedom of speech in order to make informed decisions in their use of their power in voting. In particular, Americans have complete liberty in their political views and expression. Congress may not act to restrict these freedoms such as were the effects of HUAC that were detailed in the opinions of Judges Edgerton and Charles Clark. Moreover, since the investigative powers of Congress are restricted to their areas of legislative authority, the Communist question is outside their purview.

Chandler still needed an attorney to make his argument in court. After Ginger declined, Chandler reached out further. He was impressed by a legal brief, written by two University of Chicago professors, in opposition to the hearings of the SISS. Chandler traveled to Chicago to discuss the handling of his case with the junior author, William Robert Ming Jr., a pioneering NAACP attorney.[31] They got along splendidly. Ming's "eyes lit up" at the mention of pursuing the Meiklejohn defense. Chandler believed they were "absolute soul mates."[32] It remained for Ming to discuss the arrangements with his legal partner.

The elation ended shortly after Chandler returned to Ann Arbor. Ming telephoned to say that his partner insisted on the firm charging full commercial rates for the defense. At this point, Chandler reacted in a way that he later would regret. He felt as if the financial condition was a betrayal, and he began to question Ming's commitment. Discomfort over the financial aspects

would have been easy to appreciate. Chandler was expecting
to lose his job and be blacklisted. With Natalie still in graduate
school, he was already undertaking a huge risk to his family's
welfare. The specter of even more substantial debt would have
seemed overwhelming.

legal Bill

Yet others in his circumstances took on legal bills beyond
their resources. Thus, it was more a matter of a political purity
filter than of money that soured Chandler on engaging Ming.
Sixty years later, when asked in an interview about regrets in
his life, Chandler mentioned first his missed opportunity to
have Ming represent him.[33]

Both Ginger and Ming advised Chandler that counsel was
unnecessary for him with HUAC. Chandler decided to go it
alone in the hearing and put off obtaining an attorney until the
criminal proceedings. To prepare for the HUAC interrogation, Chandler reviewed prior testimony by other professors
and went through mock sessions, questioned by Natalie and
friends.

HUAC subcommittee for the 1954 Michigan investigation:
(left to right) Gordon Scherer, Kit Clardy, and Morgan Moulder.
(PHOTO BY JIMMY TAFOYA FOR *THE DETROIT FREE PRESS*)

CHAPTER SIX

The 1954 HUAC Hearings

The three-person HUAC Subcommittee for the 1954 Michigan hearings was strikingly junior in its makeup. The Republicans, Kit Clardy of Michigan and Gordon Scherer of Ohio, were both in their first congressional term. The sole Democrat, Morgan Moulder of Missouri, was in his third.

Clardy's tenure as chair of the subcommittee was the highest-profile endeavor of his undistinguished legislative career. In his first attempt at elective office, Clardy lost in the 1950 Republican primary to the incumbent congressman William Blackney. Two years later, after Blackney served his final term, Clardy was the party nominee for his vacated seat. The *Detroit Free Press* carried campaign statements and rebuttals by Clardy and his Democratic opponent Donald Hayworth, an English professor from Michigan State, who wrote: "To follow the leadership of McCarthy is to take the trail of vigilantism."[1] Clardy, an admirer of McCarthy, responded that Hayworth "is more concerned with smearing those who have exposed Communists in government than he is rooting out subversives."

Clardy won in 1952. The 1954 HUAC hearings were an

opportunity for him to boost his standing for the rematch against Hayworth at the end of the year. It did not work. Hayworth was victorious, leaving Clardy as a one-term congressman who was then defeated in the 1956 primary.

The Clardy-chaired subcommittee held hearings in Detroit, Lansing, and Flint for their "Investigation of Communist Activities in the State of Michigan." Lawrence Klein's executive testimony took place in Detroit on April 30, 1954. Klein was fortunate that Clardy was the only member present for the session, as congressmen would at times compete to be provocative. With Klein, Clardy largely conceded the floor to committee counsel Frank Tavenner for the questioning.

Tavenner took Klein through his activities in Boston and Chicago that began with teaching in schools with left-wing ties. Klein was responsive to all questions including his CPUSA membership but could recall few names. He was never pressed. Klein's reasons for leaving the CPUSA were "I found meetings thoroughly uninteresting and dull; it was a waste of time; they did nothing." He agreed with Tavenner's suggestion that "the objectives that the Communist Party is aiming toward are wrong in principle, theory, and practice." Only then did Clardy enter the questioning, getting Klein to admit, "I was used by the Communist Party." Clardy then expressed his approval with Klein's testimony and the witness was dismissed.[2]

All of the HUAC subcommittee members were present on May 10 for the testimony by the other University of Michigan faculty and graduate students that took place in Lansing.[3] The first witness to be called was Nate Coburn, leading to a prearranged discussion. An attorney representing Coburn rose to say that his client was unable to appear due to illness. Clardy then agreed to defer Coburn's testimony, leaving the subpoena in effect.

Coburn had been going back and forth over his health with HUAC since being subpoenaed six months earlier. The committee was skeptical of Coburn's claim that he was afflicted with multiple sclerosis. By this time, a preliminary report was in from a physician with the Public Health Service. According to Tavenner, they were waiting for the final report. In fact, Coburn did have multiple sclerosis and he was not recalled. Still, Clardy found it necessary to put his name in the record.

For their testimonies, Clement Markert and Mark Nickerson arranged for a local attorney to appear with them. Markert recalled that the biggest benefit of having representation was the additional time to think through his responses during the brief intervals permitted for consultation.[4] He faced considerable questioning over his 1938 travel to fight alongside Communists in the Spanish Civil War.

Markert's path to the CPUSA began with self-radicalization while in a Pueblo, Colorado, high school. Experiencing the privations of the Great Depression, he became "hostile" to capitalism.[5] By 1935, when Markert entered the University of Colorado, he had come to regard himself as a Communist. At college he became associated with like-minded individuals.

In Spain during this period, the leftist Republicans were at war against the fascist Nationalist forces. Among CPUSA members, the pilgrimage to serve on the side of the Republicans became regarded as a heroic calling. The United States itself was neutral and discouraged its citizens from participating in Spain's civil war. In his junior year, Markert and his roommate, Edgar Merrick, left college to join the battle against the Francisco Franco–led Nationalists in Spain.[6] Unable to obtain passports, Markert and Merrick stowed away on a freighter to France. They then made their way to the war in Spain. The casualty rate among Americans was high in their Abraham Lincoln Brigade. Markert survived, but Merrick went missing and was presumed dead.

Following the defeat of the Republicans, Markert was repatriated to the United States. He returned to the University of Colorado, graduating with highest honors in 1940. Then

Markert began graduate study at UCLA, which he aborted when the United States entered the Second World War. Again, Markert felt compelled to do what he could to stop the advance of fascism. His attempt, a few days after Pearl Harbor, to enlist in the United States military was unsuccessful.[7] After contributing to the war effort as a welder at a shipyard, Markert was accepted into the Merchant Marine. Following the war, he studied biology at Johns Hopkins, completing a PhD in 1948. Prior to beginning his position at the University of Michigan, Markert engaged in postdoctoral research at the California Institute of Technology with geneticist and future Nobel Prize–winner George Beadle. Through much of the 1940s, Markert was a member of the CPUSA.

FBI files on Markert, obtained under a Freedom of Information Act request,[8] reveal that the Bureau maintained a long-term interest in his political activity. The first report on him in their records came from a confidential informant on September 15, 1941, who alleged that Markert was in charge of the Young Communist League in Pueblo. A deliberate investigation began the following year.

In Pueblo, an FBI agent made inquiries that included interviews with the high school principal and Edgar Merrick's mother. Mrs. Merrick asserted that Markert had persuaded her son to join him in traveling to Spain to fight in the civil war. The principal told the agent that Markert had graduated from the University of Colorado and was presently living in California.[9] Next, at the University of Colorado, another agent spoke with a sociology professor who had taught Markert and believed him to be a "professional Communist." The professor added that Markert was "brilliant but unsettled" and "a very dangerous individual."[10]

The trail led to Los Angeles where the investigation of Markert intensified in 1943. Now he was under consideration for the *custodial detention* index.[11] Custodial detention was a surveillance program of dubious legality begun by FBI director J. Edgar Hoover in 1939.[12] With the Second World War underway in Europe, Hoover was compiling a list of both aliens and citizens whose loyalty to the United States might be questionable if the United States were to enter the hostilities. In particular, the index was a mechanism for keeping tabs on members of the CPUSA.

The initial investigation of Markert in Los Angeles turned up little.[13] Interviews in visits to his current and previous residences yielded nothing of consequence. One lead came from his draft board. Markert had obtained a permit to work in Honduras for a Pan-American contractor. A check with the company revealed that Markert was never hired because his passport application had been rejected. A request was sent to Washington to explore the passport situation while a mail cover was begun to monitor his correspondents and their addresses. All of this took place in February.

April brought the first significant links to the CPUSA.[14] Through its "trash cover maintained on CP Headquarters LA, Calif."[15] the FBI obtained a copy of Markert's transfer card between CPUSA branches. A comprehensive search of Markert's apartment identified a wide range of Communist materials. The FBI account does not reveal how access to the dwelling was obtained, merely listing the source as "highly confidential." For some period, Markert was even being followed. A report details his driving to the residence of a suspected Communist couple where he left a dinner invitation on the door. That evening a car with the other couple's license plate was observed parked in front of the Markert home. Finally, information was obtained through another government agency that a few months earlier Markert was denied a passport to work on the Pan-American Highway due to his participation in the Spanish Civil War. The FBI also gained access to details on his illegal 1938 travel to Spain.

In June, Markert was placed in the custodial detention index at the lower threat level of C.[16] Five weeks later, the attorney

Breaking / tools / misc

general, Francis Biddle, ordered J. Edgar Hoover to shut down the index, admonishing the Director: "There is no statutory authorization or other present justification for keeping a 'custodial detention' list of citizens. The Department fulfills its proper functions by investigating the activities of persons who may have violated the law. It is not aided in this work by classifying persons as to dangerousness."[17] Hoover did terminate the program, but in a move of brazen insubordination and lawlessness created a new off-the-books index for the same suspects and information under the classification "security matter."

In their investigation of Markert, the FBI was the beneficiary of information supplied from other government departments. Not only were agents permitted to review Markert's passport file upon request in 1943, but in 1945 a revealing transcript was forwarded to the FBI at the initiative of the Office of Naval Intelligence.[18] To become a radio operator in the Merchant Marine, Markert had undergone an interview about his political activity. In the transcript, Markert affirmed that he was currently a believer in communism and that, excluding his time in the Merchant Marine, had been active in proselytizing the movement since his days as an undergraduate. Markert's admission in the interview that he had served as executive secretary of the San Pedro CPUSA branch would resurface in his HUAC hearing.

After the Second World War, Markert reconnected with the CPUSA, but began to scale back his involvement. During the 1945–48 period that he was working on his PhD at Johns Hopkins, the Baltimore FBI office received no intelligence on current Communist activity by Markert.[19] In 1951, however, one informant came forward to report that Markert had been in the CPUSA when he was at Johns Hopkins, and another to say that he was at least sympathetic to their cause.[20]

With Markert's move to the California Institute of Technology in 1948, the Los Angeles bureau of the FBI resumed oversight of his case. On April 13, 1949, a memo from the Los Angeles office to the Director about Markert simply stated: "The Security Index card being maintained on this individual has been tabbed 'dangerous.'" A handwritten notation, presumably from the headquarters office, adds the words "tab DETCOM." DETCOM was a clandestine FBI list of Communists to be arrested in the event of war with the Soviet Union.[21]

Several subsequent reports confirmed the DETCOM designation.[22] The only suspicious activity detected by the Los Angeles bureau was Markert's membership on the Executive Board of the Hollywood Arts, Sciences, and Professions Council.[23] Despite its innocuous name, this organization, which included members of the Hollywood Ten and other Communists, was under FBI surveillance.[24]

After assuming his assistant professorship at the University of Michigan in 1950, Markert refrained from political activity, concentrating his energy on scientific work. The Detroit bureau's preliminary investigation, through their university informants, determined that Markert was the project director of a grant from the Atomic Energy Commission.[25] Noting the DETCOM classification and CPUSA priors in his file, Detroit proposed undertaking an investigation into possible espionage. Washington ordered a more suitable Security Matter-C inquiry.[26] The subsequent probe, including a mail cover and interview with a faculty colleague, did not reveal any contemporaneous subversive activity.

The basis for HUAC's 1953 attention on Markert was a succinct summary of his file from the FBI, depicting a long-term Communist.[27] The conspicuous feature of the report was Markert's combat in the Spanish Civil War. Without compromising its confidential sources, the FBI listed four organizations documenting his subversive memberships throughout the 1940s. To back up their case for the hearing, HUAC investigators obtained copies of the paperwork on Markert's 1938 applications for a passport and repatriation.

The questioning of Markert began with a recital of his educational and employment history. When he reached his service as a radio operator in the Merchant Marine, counsel Tavenner asked Markert if he was a CPUSA member at that time. It was a tricky question. Tavenner was addressing a brief period when Markert was not in the Party, but a forthright denial by him may have waived his right to use the Fifth Amendment. Markert declined to answer, citing the First Amendment. Clardy then intervened to clarify whether Markert was invoking the Fifth Amendment as well. After some back and forth in which Clardy refused to concede that the First Amendment was an acceptable non-response, Markert added the Fifth Amendment to his invocation.

What followed was considerable sparring over whether Markert participated in the Spanish Civil War. The subcommittee attempted to have Markert confirm that a photostatic copy of his passport application was genuine. Markert would only concede that the signature and photograph bore substantial resemblance to his own. On other questions, Markert took the Fifth or claimed an imperfect memory of events sixteen years earlier. The questioning took on elements of a game.

When asked whether he had belonged to each of the four organizations from the FBI list, Markert pleaded the Fifth Amendment. The irony was that not only was he actually willing to answer these questions (if it did not waive his future use of the Fifth Amendment), but the subcommittee already had the information. Driving Markert's testimony was his desire to protect himself from prosecution for withholding names. The subcommittee sought to ensure that he would be blacklisted for doing so, and thus serve as an object lesson for future witnesses contemplating an unfriendly approach.

The examination of Nickerson was similar to that of Markert, with a slight twist. When asked if he was a member of the Communist Party at a particular time, Nickerson's First Amendment response apparently was unnoticed by members of the subcommittee. His next use of the First Amendment was challenged by Clardy, leading to a supplement of the Fifth Amendment by Nickerson to both, and numerous future, questions. Neither Markert nor Nickerson were cited for contempt.

Chandler fully expected his testimony to be the basis for an indictment. Hoping that the case would reach a review by the Supreme Court, his responses were especially important. Yet in his rehearsals with Natalie and friends, they could only speculate on what from his past might raise questions. Certainly, HUAC would be aware of the confiscation of his passport. Did they also know of his role in organizing faculty to protest the restrictions on Michigan speakers?

The report to HUAC, by the FBI, on Chandler began with his passport and ended with his involvement with *Operation Mind*.[28] Between were a number of connections to allegedly subversive people, activities, and organizations in Boston and Ann Arbor. Much of the information was from informants, particularly Irving Rozian, Chandler's assiduous friend from the Council of Arts, Sciences, and Professions.

Before examining his testimony, it will be useful to note several things. Chandler was twenty-seven years old with one year remaining on his contract as an instructor. Natalie was in the first trimester of her second pregnancy[29] and midway through her study as a doctoral student. Chandler entered the hearing feeling challenged, as if he were in an athletic competition.[30] He needed to be careful in deciding which questions to answer and when to assert the First Amendment, always attentive to seemingly innocuous questions that might bait him into more sensitive explorations. Generally, the objective of the subcommittee was to elicit responses of two sorts, political views and associations. Chandler was prepared for both.

(THE COMPLETE TESTIMONY OF CHANDLER DAVIS IS AVAILABLE AT HTTPS://MONTHLYREVIEW.ORG/CHANDLERDAVIS).

Early on, Tavenner asked Chandler if, in his undergraduate days at Harvard, he was aware of the existence of a CPUSA student branch on campus. Note that Tavenner was not asking the

Communist question. For Chandler, it was close enough to his political associations for him to respond that, under the protections of the First Amendment, Tavenner's inquiry was beyond the purview of a congressional committee. Clardy then permitted Chandler to state his Meiklejohn-inspired justification. As with Nickerson, the Fifth Amendment did not arise immediately. When Scherer eventually asked whether he was asserting the Fifth Amendment, Chandler made clear that the Fifth Amendment was not a part of his testimony.

Despite the pressure and the intimidation from HUAC, Chandler remained faithful to his game plan. Moreover, he accomplished what he set out to do. With the expected indictment for contempt of Congress, he would be in a position to claim standing for a First Amendment challenge to the legality of the HUAC hearings.

Chandler did provide one opinion of a political nature in stating his "oppos[ition] to violent revolution as a means of achieving political change." Making the response was arguably inconsistent with Chandler's objection to the proceedings. Nevertheless, it did fortify him with a good talking point for subsequent rounds of the battle.

Operation Mind was the dominant topic of Chandler's questioning. The subcommittee had a copy of the pamphlet and knew of the informant's disclosure that Chandler had arranged for the printing. At least Scherer and Tavenner drew the incorrect inference that Chandler was the anonymous author. Their efforts to coax a confession confirmed for Chandler that the HUAC intelligence was flawed. He resisted the temptation to set them straight as it would have violated his First Amendment principle and could have exposed Natalie to jeopardy.

Chandler was surprised by how little HUAC seemed to be aware of his past activity, remarking, "I didn't get credit for all that I had done."[31] For example, nothing was asked about his initiative in organizing faculty opposition to the constraints on campus speakers. One area of inquiry was totally unexpected. Clardy asked, "if it is not a fact that you were a friend of Gerhart Eisler." Eisler was a major figure in the international Communist movement who was convicted for refusing to cooperate in a HUAC investigation.[32] He fled the United States in 1949 while out on bail for his appeal.

Clardy's question about Eisler was undoubtedly motivated by the FBI report to HUAC that stated in 1949 that Chandler "was a personal friend of Gerhart Eisler." Yet Chandler had no recollection of ever meeting Eisler. He did know that Natalie had received an autographed copy of a book from Eisler when she attended a talk by him at Smith or Harvard. She had also disposed of the gift after his defection and prior to the Davises leaving Cambridge in 1950.[33]

Even with the benefit of the FBI files that were made available, the Eisler question remains puzzling. There is only one (non-redacted) reference to Eisler in Chandler's files.[34] In 1952 the informant from the Council of Arts, Sciences, and Professions reported that Chandler possessed an autographed copy of a book by Eisler. While it is understandable that the tense may have gotten lost in transmission, it remains a considerable jump from possession in 1952 to friendship three years earlier. Several explanations are possible. After the hearing, Chandler and Natalie suspected that the FBI was searching their garbage in Cambridge. Alternatively, an informant may have observed the book gift and made a report to the FBI. In either case, the intelligence may not have been included in the material provided under the Freedom of Information Act request.

While the University of Michigan would commence employment reviews immediately on Davis, Markert, and Nickerson, the legal track for Chandler developed more slowly. As his case proceeded through the courts, it became intertwined with those of two other uncooperative HUAC witnesses whose hearings were sandwiched around Chandler's in the preceding and succeeding

months. Since the contempt cases of John Watkins and Lloyd
Barenblatt would reach the Supreme Court and establish important precedents, some background on their HUAC hearings will
be useful for readers.

John Watkins's pre-HUAC biography offered little indication of a destiny that would intersect that of Chandler's.[35]
Watkins grew up in the Midwest where his formal education
ended in the eighth grade. For the next decade, he worked at
a variety of farm and construction jobs. In the midst of the
Depression, Watkins began employment as a machine operator for International Harvester in East Moline. At International
Harvester he became an active union member in the Farm
Equipment Workers (FE). In 1942, Watkins embarked on an
extended leave from his company to serve in the rough-and-
tumble world as a union official for the left-linked FE.[36] As
labor federations battled to gain affiliations with individual
unions, the FE was then under the jurisdiction of the Congress
of Industrial Organizations (CIO).

By the time Watkins was subpoenaed to testify in Washington
before HUAC, his East Moline FE local was an affiliate of the
anti-Communist United Auto Workers (UAW). The position
of UAW president Walter Reuther was to support the legal
defense of its members before congressional committees,
provided they did not invoke the Fifth Amendment.[37] The
HUAC subcommittee examining Watkins included Scherer
and Moulder as well as chair Harold Velde and James Frazier.
Two union adversaries, Donald Spencer and Walter Rumsey,
previously had testified that Watkins recruited them into the
CPUSA. In responding to the Communist question, Watkins
made the following statement:

> I am not now nor have I ever been a card-carrying member of
> the Communist Party. Rumsey was wrong when he said I had
> recruited him into the Party, that I had received his dues, that I
> paid dues to him, and that I had used the alias Sam Brown.

Spencer was wrong when he termed any meetings which I attended as closed Communist Party meetings.

I would like to make it clear that for a period of time from approximately 1942 to 1947 I cooperated with the Communist Party and participated in Communist activities to such a degree that some persons may honestly believe that I was a member of the Party.

I have made contributions upon occasions to Communist causes. I have signed petitions for Communist causes. I attended caucuses at an FE convention at which Communist Party officials were present.

Since I freely cooperated with the Communist Party, I have no motive for making the distinction between cooperation and membership except the simple fact that it is the truth. I never carried a Communist Party card. I never accepted discipline and indeed on several occasions I opposed their position.

Asked what motive Rumsey and Spencer may have had to implicate him, Watkins replied that he had expelled both from the union. Then, upon request, Watkins named a few CPUSA members. When asked to confirm other names provided by Rumsey, Watkins made another prepared statement:

I would like to get one thing perfectly clear, Mr. Chairman. I am not going to plead the Fifth Amendment, but I refuse to answer certain questions that I believe are outside the proper scope of your committee's activities. I will answer any questions which this committee puts to me about myself. I will also answer questions about those persons whom I knew to be members of the Communist Party and whom I believe still are. I will not, however, answer any questions with respect to others with whom I associated in the past. I do not believe that any law in this country requires me to testify about persons who may in the past have been Communist Party members or otherwise engaged in Communist Party activity but who to my best knowledge and belief have long since removed themselves from the Communist movement.

I do not believe that such questions are relevant to the work of this committee nor do I believe that this committee has the right to undertake the public exposure of persons because of their past activities. I may be wrong, and the committee may have this power, but until and unless a court of law so holds and directs me to answer, I most firmly refuse to discuss the political activities of my past associates.

Upon further questioning, Watkins confirmed that he was "not in any way raising the Fifth Amendment." Watkins maintained his position over a long list of names that Rumsey previously had provided. Throughout his testimony, Watkins made no specific mention of the First Amendment.

In a case with many similarities to Chandler's, Lloyd Barenblatt testified before HUAC in Washington on June 28, 1954.[38] Three years older than Chandler, Barenblatt was raised in the Depression-era Bronx by Russian-Jewish parents.[39] His undergraduate education at the City College of New York was followed by voluntary service in the Army Air Force during the Second World War.

After the war, Barenblatt concluded that the CPUSA positions on civil rights and other issues aligned well with his own. As a graduate student at the University of Michigan in the late 1940s, he joined the Haldane Club, a local branch of the CPUSA for graduate students. Without completing a PhD, Barenblatt left Ann Arbor in 1950 to become an instructor of psychology at Vassar College. He remained in the CPUSA until 1952, leaving out of disenchantment with the movement and its policies.

Two weeks prior to his 1954 hearing, and two weeks after receiving his HUAC subpoena, Barenblatt's Vassar contract expired and was not renewed. This left him unemployed as he contemplated whether to assert the Fifth Amendment. As with Chandler, Barenblatt learned of Meiklejohn's freedom of speech philosophy and enthusiastically adopted the First Amendment approach over the Fifth. He prepared a long statement, with

Supreme Court precedents, as a response for any question about his political and religious beliefs, personal and private affairs, and associational activities.

Barenblatt was unaware of how his name had come to the attention of HUAC. The mystery was solved by the first witness on the day of his hearing. The committee counsel prefaced the testimony of Francis Crowley with some explanatory remarks. One year earlier Crowley had appeared before the committee under subpoena. He refused to answer any questions. After his recent indictment, Crowley had expressed regret over his previous posture and requested a second opportunity to be forthright with the committee. He was about to testify under his own initiative.

Crowley, a former Army buddy and college roommate of Barenblatt, had also been a member of the Haldane Club. Barenblatt listened to his, up to that instant, friend's testimony. Crowley explained that he "s[aw] no reason for my suffering a penalty for something that I no longer believe in." Later he explained that he was influenced by the change in his responsibilities over the past year, having married and now expecting a child. Crowley went on to name many names and confirm that Barenblatt had been a member of the Haldane Club. The additional information that Barenblatt's view had changed and that he was no longer a member of the CPUSA was of little interest to the committee.

Shortly into Barenblatt's testimony, the counsel asked, "Were you a member of the Haldane Club of the Communist Party at Michigan?" Barenblatt's attempt to read his statement of objection was cut off. A long dispute ensued over whether Barenblatt would be permitted to read the statement. During this discussion, the question changed from the Haldane Club to a version of the Communist question. After Barenblatt stipulated that he was not relying on the Fifth Amendment, his statement was grudgingly placed in the record without being read.

Barenblatt later reflected on his own reaction to Crowley's testimony:

Well, I never suspected that Crowley could do anything like that until the day I appeared before the committee. They put him on a stage with his back to the audience. When he mentioned my name, I was stunned! His betrayal was unimaginable to me. Looking back, I had many clues that he might be going that way, that I refused to believe. I myself was very critical of the Communist Party, both from the standpoint of democratic principles and human rights and their lack of understanding of American equalitarian and democratic feelings. It was just plain stupidity! Dissidents in Europe at that time faced torture, faced death. People were running scared in this country—not only the fear of losing their job, but the greatest fear was the opprobrium of your neighbors, from your own family. That's what scared people more than anything else. I remember many conversations with Crowley about this, but it never occurred to me that he was preparing to use this to justify his informer act.[40]

Congress approved contempt citations for Watkins and Crowley on May 11, 1954, and for Davis and Barenblatt on July 23. Following his testimony, HUAC decided that Crowley had purged himself of contempt.

Harlan Hatcher, 1957.

CHAPTER SEVEN

University of Michigan Reviews

President Harlan Hatcher listened to a radio broadcast of the May 10 HUAC hearing and moved swiftly to respond on behalf of the University of Michigan.[1] Within two hours of the subcommittee's adjournment, Hatcher released a statement that he was suspending Davis, Markert, and Nickerson pending an investigation.[2] Meanwhile, the three faculty members were informed, by messenger, of their immediate suspensions with pay.

In reviewing the subsequent inquiry by the University of Michigan, a valuable resource is the report of an American Association of University Professors (AAUP) investigating committee that made a site visit to the Ann Arbor campus at the end of 1956.[3] One of the AAUP Report conclusions was that the summary suspensions, prior to investigation, were unjustified under the university's "good cause" provisions protecting against immediate damage from faculty carrying on their responsibilities.[4]

The next issue for Davis, Markert, and Nickerson was to determine their postures for the university investigation. Markert and Nickerson had reluctantly relied on the Fifth

AAUP

Amendment with HUAC as the only course that permitted them to avoid both naming names and going to prison.
In the university phase, the consequences were professional
rather than criminal, removing the Fifth Amendment waiver
doctrine as a consideration. These circumstances permitted
Markert and Nickerson to follow the course they would have
preferred with HUAC, to answer forthrightly about their own
pasts without incurring a legal obligation to implicate others.

Adopting the cooperative approach of Markert and
Nickerson with the University review undoubtedly would have
enhanced Chandler's slim prospects for a favorable outcome.
Yet, since being urged by Hatcher to follow the AAU guidance
in his testimony, Chandler had come to view the university as
an appendage of HUAC.[5] Furthermore, the same principles
of political freedom and protection of unpopular opinions in
public life were also applicable under the notion of academic
freedom. Chandler decided that the university was not entitled
to inquire and pass judgment on his political views. It was a
rare instance of variance with Natalie, who, at the time, preferred that her husband cooperate at least to the extent of
stating that he was not presently a member of the CPUSA.[6]

Serious defects emerged, from the beginning, with the
University of Michigan investigative process. The review
procedures were set out in Section 5.10 of the University
Bylaws.[7] "Grounds for dismissal" were to be stated in "reasonable particularity." The faculty member was provided with
a twenty-day period in which to request a review by a panel
in his or her college. If the decision by the panel was adverse,
twenty days after the issuance of a report were allowed for
submission of an appeal to the Senate Advisory Committee
(SAC). The SAC recommendation was to be transmitted to
the university president, who, in turn, advised the Board of
Regents for final action.

As mentioned in chapter 5, during the previous spring
President Hatcher had pitched the AAU statement to the

faculty as a policy for dealing with HUAC matters that he argued required urgent resolution to protect the reputation of the university. Rather than accepting the controversial AAU policy, the faculty Senate devised a supplemental Section 5.101 to address Hatcher's concerns by expediting cases such as the current ones.[8] The new regulation allowed for the president to initiate the dismissal, reduced the waiting period to five days and the number of hearing tribunals to just one, the SAC or its designee, all the while requiring that "the provisions of Section 5.10 shall be followed as far as applicable" with stated exceptions. In February, the SAC appointed a subcommittee on Intellectual Freedom and Integrity to serve in the role as the hearing committee. The AAUP Report referred to this five-person committee, chaired by psychology professor Angus Campbell, as the Bylaw Committee.

Thus, at the time of the May 10 hearing there existed three duly constituted review committees pertinent to the bylaws. The Executive Committee of the College of Literature, Science, and the Arts (for Davis and Markert)[9] and the SAC were the two tribunals under Section 5.10 and the Bylaw Committee was the designee under Section 5.101. Chandler could expect to undergo a hearing before either the Executive or the Bylaw Committee.

According to a later statement of Dean Charles Odegaard and the Executive Committee, "On Monday evening, May 10, at the request of the President, the Dean informed the members of the Executive Committee that the President . . . as a preliminary step before taking any further action in any direction, wished to consult with us and the chairmen of the two departments concerned. To prepare ourselves for this consultation, it appeared necessary to hear the testimony before the Clardy Committee in so far as the two members of our faculty were concerned, and if possible, to hear whatever Messrs. Davis and Markert were willing to tell us about the matter from their point of view."[10]

The Executive Committee statement went on to report that on the following day they and the chairs of mathematics and zoology listened to a tape recording of the hearing. On Wednesday, Davis and Markert appeared separately before the committee and their respective chairs. The meetings with Davis and Markert were, in fact, an investigative step. In these sessions, both witnesses disclosed information that they had withheld from HUAC. It is unclear from the record whether President Hatcher authorized what turned into interrogations.[11]

In his approximately one-hour session with the Executive Committee, Markert thoroughly reviewed his CPUSA history, volunteering connections that had not arisen during the HUAC hearing.[12] He described his energetic participation in the CPUSA as an undergraduate after coming to believe, during the Depression, that capitalism had failed. Then, Markert explained that after remaining active for several additional years, he began drifting away from the Party during his time in graduate school at Johns Hopkins, with no involvement since coming to Michigan in 1950. Markert was careful to point out that his departure resulted not so much from a change in his own beliefs as it was his perception that the Party and its personnel were becoming less independent and more controlled from abroad.

Odegaard described Chandler's approach before the Executive Committee as follows:

Davis took the position with the College Executive Committee, which was comparable to the position he took with the Clardy Committee, saying that if six months ago, prior to the receipt of his subpoena, any number [member] of the faculty had talked to him about political matters, he would have talked freely about his political beliefs, but that ever since he received the subpoena, he has felt he was on trial for his political beliefs, and so in a sense he is standing on the rights of privacy for them, claiming that the First Amendment gives him constitutional protection.[13]

One new piece of information was disclosed by Davis in the hour-long session. In an effort to impeach the credibility of HUAC and its sources, Chandler informed the Executive Committee that he had never met Gerhart Eisler.[14] The investigation continued on Thursday. The two department chairs, accompanied by a member of the departmental leadership, appeared before the Executive Committee.

Odegaard later reported that by this time on Thursday the Executive Committee "ha[d] spent many hours in reviewing the cases on the evidence and impressions gained up to May 13th. In discussing them it endeavored to reach general conclusions on the basic issues in the two cases."[15] The Executive Committee was "convinced of the competence and objectivity" of both men as scholars and teachers. They believed in Markert's "moral integrity" and decided that he was within his rights in his use of the Fifth Amendment. The Executive Committee also was satisfied that Markert had not been a CPUSA member for some time. They "conclude[d] that he should be reinstated as soon as possible."

The findings on Davis were more qualified. They disagreed with his conduct before HUAC, but believed that he was sincere in his First Amendment claim, which was, in itself, a matter under litigation. They regretted Chandler's lack of cooperation with their committee and distinguished him from Markert on the CPUSA issue. "In the absence of proof Davis is a member of that party we must in all justice assume that he is not." The bottom line was "We conclude that we do not find in his conduct before the Clardy Committee or as a member of the University any ground on which he can justly be dismissed. We hope that a firmer basis of judgment may be forthcoming, but we believe that he should be reinstated unless conclusive evidence is found of his unfitness to be a member of the faculty."

It was then, on Thursday afternoon, May 13, that the Dean and the Executive Committee met with Hatcher for the consultation the president had requested three days earlier as a preliminary step in his deciding on the direction of the investigation.[16] In the interim, the Executive Committee had conducted a substantial inquiry and reached tentative conclusions that they confidentially shared with the president. With the knowledge that the Executive Committee was likely to recommend reinstatement, President Hatcher decided to designate the Bylaw Committee instead for conducting the investigation of record.

The wording of Section 5.101, however, left some ambiguity as to the precise role of the Bylaw Committee.[17] To Hatcher's chagrin, the Bylaw Committee viewed its function as one that would hear appeals from faculty on dismissal decisions already made by the president. Intending to have the Bylaw Committee act in an advisory rather than appeal capacity, Hatcher unsuccessfully sought intervention from the Dean of the Law School. The Dean advised that the Bylaw Committee had "a possible, though not a necessary or helpful interpretation."

Following through with the prevailing reading of Section 5.101, Hatcher could have initiated dismissal, leaving five days for appeals to the Bylaw Committee. Hatcher did not take this course, which would have placed him in a troublesome position. Although the Army-McCarthy hearings that soon would lead to Senator McCarthy's demise were underway, the second Red Scare would survive him. In view of public sentiment, Hatcher regarded the actions of Davis, Markert, and Nickerson as damaging to the welfare of the University. Yet on campus, there was considerable support for the three professors. Hatcher wanted some cover, such as a faculty recommendation, in moving for their dismissal.

The fast-tracking Section 5.101 stated, "the provisions of Section 5.10 shall be followed as far as applicable," making the Executive Committee an investigative option that was within the bylaws. The problem for Hatcher was, as we shall see, that the recommendation he could expect from the Executive Committee would not be the outcome he desired. Left with the option of two unpalatable courses within the bylaws, he decided to create a new step in the process. Hatcher asked the SAC to appoint a special committee to conduct an investigation and advise him on an action.[18] SAC obliged on May 20 by appointing a five-person Special Advisory Committee, chaired by Russell Smith of the Law School, that the AAUP Report refers to as the Ad Hoc Committee. The process became the sequence of an investigation and recommendation by the Ad Hoc Committee, a decision by the president, a possible appeal to the Bylaw Committee, reconsideration by the president, and then a final decision by the Regents.

Surprisingly, the extrajudicial role of the Ad Hoc Committee and the prejudicial marginalization of the Executive Committee investigation went uncriticized in the AAUP Report. That is not to say that the report was silent on failings by university authorities. One of its recurring complaints was that "[n]o statement setting forth, with reasonable particularity, proposed grounds of dismissal was furnished to the Ad Hoc Committee or to the suspended men."[19] The closest action to fulfilling this bylaw safeguard were statements presented by President Hatcher and the Ad Hoc Committee chair at a May 31 meeting to rehearse procedures with Davis, Markert, and Nickerson. Hatcher declared:

> This is not an inquiry into the technical competency of the men in question. It does not involve any question of the right freely to investigate, to arrive at or to hold unpopular views. It is a question of relation to or involvement in a conspiratorial movement which, if successful, would subvert the freedoms and the liberties which we hold sacred.[20]

No relation to teaching

He then went on to quote from the AAU statement and closed with examples of questions on CPUSA membership that required answers. The Ad Hoc Committee's statement added little as to particular grounds for dismissal.

1. To put the matter as precisely as possible, we conceive it to be our duty to determine whether your status with the University should be terminated because of any or all of the following:

(1) Your relationship, present or past, with the communist party or with communist activities; (2) your response to questions put to you recently by the Clardy Committee; or (3) your responses to questions which we shall put to you in the course of our proceedings. We do not propose to inquire into your technical proficiency in your respective fields, or your teaching or research ability, for our understanding is that no question has been raised with respect to these matters. . . .

3. We have stated that one factor which of necessity will have to be taken into account is the attitude which each of you takes with respect to the work of this committee. We earnestly hope that you will be open and candid with us when we ask questions intended to give us information concerning your present and past relationship with the communist party or with communist activities, and concerning your reasons for certain of your responses put to you by the Clardy Committee.[21]

From the statements by the president and the Ad Hoc Committee, it was clear that both regarded current membership in the CPUSA as grounds for dismissal. What other relationships with the Party were sufficient for termination, and which of these were alleged to be held by the three faculty? Not only were the answers to these questions unstated with any particularity but apparently they were under ongoing consideration.

The AAUP Report also noted the violation of a bylaw provision that restricted the investigation to consideration of evidence made part of the case record.[22] On June 2, President

Hatcher and the Ad Hoc Committee met with HUAC investigator Donald Appell. No transcript was maintained, but some off-the-record notes were located in a "Working Materials" folder.[23] An explanatory paragraph stated that Appell did not disclose sources, but he asserted that all of the HUAC questions at the hearing were well grounded. Among the notes were statements that Davis "knew Eisler intimately and personally as a friend," "was an active Communist at Harvard," and "that he has been active member of c.p. since coming to Ann Arbor." As Davis had not been a member of the Party for a year, both Hatcher and the Ad Hoc Committee were left to decide the weight of an incorrect, inadmissible, and damning allegation.

The meeting with Appell was not an isolated incident. The Ad Hoc Committee report reveals that they conducted an additional off-the-record session with an unnamed person from an unspecified government agency. "Certain of the facts alleged by this investigator [Appell] have been alleged by another government investigator whom this Committee interviewed."[24] The surreptitious FBI seems an unlikely source, particularly as there is no mention of such cooperation in Chandler's FBI file. The most probable origin of the confirming intelligence was the Michigan State Police, whose "Red Squad" surveilled and harassed the Ann Arbor left. In one case at this time, the Red Squad successfully prevailed upon a Michigan dean to terminate the teaching assistantship of mathematics graduate student Steve Smale, who was suspected of being a CPUSA member.[25]

The Ad Hoc Committee, prior to interviewing Davis, Markert, and Nickerson, consulted separately with the Executive Committees of their colleges and departments. The Executive Committee of the College of Literature, Science, and the Arts reported on their meetings with Davis and Markert and their conclusions that both should be reinstated. While participation in the conversation was broad, the principal contributors were Dean Odegaard, communicating the information that had been received from the faculty, and Chairman Smith, seeking additional details.[26]

The report on the Executive Committee discussion about Markert brought out their respect for his candor. The attitude toward Davis was more mixed with some frustration for his having provided less responsive answers than were desired. Members of the Executive Committee felt that firing Davis required a burden of proof that had not been met. One surprise for the Ad Hoc Committee was the revelation of Chandler's claim to have never met Eisler. Hatcher and Smith, who recognized the irreconcilable conflict with the statement of Appell, both followed up for confirmation.[27]

HUAC

IIe   In contrast, the Executive Committee of the Medical School presented a negative view of Nickerson, whose political evolution was strikingly similar to that of Markert's.[28] Nickerson had become radicalized while working in an Oregon lumber camp during the mid-1930s. He was a dues-paying member of the CPUSA as a doctoral student at Johns Hopkins from 1941 to 1944. Nickerson's Party activity continued at the University of Utah where he received a medical degree and became a rising star in pharmacology. During the late 1940s, Nickerson began to drift away from the CPUSA, largely because his scientific work consumed all of his time. When he came to Michigan in 1951 as a tenured associate professor, Nickerson was no longer a CPUSA member, but he could provide no proof of his exit.

At the meeting with the Ad Hoc Committee, Dean Albert Furstenberg of the Medical School pointed to a deviousness in Nickerson's responses. The dean was troubled by Nickerson's unwillingness to recant Communist beliefs. The chair in pharmacology, Maurice Seevers, expressed simmering grievances that were outside the HUAC inquiry. He depicted Nickerson as an arrogant and anti-authority troublemaker who sought advancement through efforts that were detrimental to his associates. Toward the end of the session,

Seevers alluded to a matter of Nickerson's integrity for which the disclosure might jeopardize industrial confidences. In the end, Seevers decided the incident was sufficiently sensitive that he would communicate it directly to President Hatcher.[29]

Interviews several decades later reveal a different perspective on the Seevers-Nickerson relationship. For his part, Nickerson recalled Seevers as arrogant and authoritarian with a "considerable ego."[30] In universities, it is not uncommon for conflicts to develop between established chairs and talented younger faculty whose ambitions they construe presumptuous. In this case, David Bohr, a Medical School associate professor who interacted scientifically with Nickerson, averred that Seevers had difficulty in coping with the prominence of the outspoken Nickerson.[31]

The discussions with the college Executive Committees gave the Ad Hoc Committee political profiles of Markert and Nickerson as unrepentant, former CPUSA members. The Communist connections that Appell alleged of Davis remained unverified. On June 8, the Ad Hoc Committee met with the Executive Committee of the mathematics department and four colleagues who had intersected with Davis in various ways. Smith addressed the mathematicians:

> We would like to have each of you relate the nature and circumstances of your contacts with the individual in question, and to the extent that you can do so, give us the substance of any information which such individual may have given you concerning his past or present affiliation, if any, with Communist activities.[32]

What Smith received were ringing endorsements of Chandler as a sincere man of principle and integrity. Those who speculated on the CPUSA issue stated that they did not believe Chandler was a current Party member. The one person present with actual knowledge of Chandler's CPUSA

Op. Mind?

116 THE PROSECUTION OF PROFESSOR CHANDLER DAVIS

status, Sumner Myers,[33] did not comment on this topic but strenuously objected to the line of questioning, threatening to leave the meeting.[34]

Mathematics department chair T. H. Hildebrandt did express discomfort with Chandler's leftist activities. The undertakings he detailed, leafleting to promote a 1952 Paul Robeson appearance in Ann Arbor and placing copies of *Operation Mind* in faculty mailboxes, were not the evidence of Communist pursuits the Smith Committee was seeking. Vice President Marvin Niehuss, who like Hatcher sat in on some of the conferences, tried out an argument that would leverage the Appell intelligence to shift the burden of proof to Chandler:

> Would your opinion be any different if it could be established with reasonable certainty that he had been a member of the Party? Would you then think that there was any burden upon him to go forward with proof that he was not now, assuming what I do assume, that present membership in the Communist Party is ground for disqualification, but assuming you establish membership, would there then be any burden upon him to speak up, or might he still maintain properly his position?[35]

Rather than gaining traction, Niehuss's query evoked doubts from the mathematicians about the credibility of what they inferred must be evidence from HUAC. Employing the Appell testimony in the manner presented by Niehuss, however, did resonate with the Smith Committee and would figure prominently in their final report.

The session with the mathematicians did nothing to lessen the conflict that was building for Chandler's hearing before the Ad Hoc Committee on June 15. At their preliminary meeting two weeks earlier, the Ad Hoc Committee made clear that they expected Chandler to answer their questions about his relationship with the CPUSA. They also left open the option of providing a written statement. Chandler followed up, attempting, in advance of his testimony, to open an alternative channel.

In his statement, Chandler began by explaining his refusal to answer questions from HUAC about political beliefs and personal associations.[36] He provided, in some detail, a Meiklejohn-inspired argument on freedom of speech. After reiterating his opposition to "violence as a means of achieving political change," Chandler offered a nuanced argument to preempt the demand for details on his CPUSA affiliations. He conceded that questions about his integrity were pertinent to the inquiry. While the CPUSA regarded itself as a political organization, others associated it with violence and attributes that bore on integrity. Chandler suggested that the Ad Hoc Committee interrogate him directly on these "impl[ied]" questions. This type of reasoning— shifting the question—so familiar to mathematicians, is referred to as a *logical argument*. He went on to explain that answering the objectionable HUAC questions when put by the Ad Hoc Committee was, in effect, being forced by HUAC to answer *their* questions.

In attendance at Chandler's Ad Hoc Committee hearing were Hatcher, Niehuss, Hildebrandt, and Wilfred Kaplan, a mathematics professor who was supportive of Chandler. The discussion became largely a dialogue between Davis and Russell Smith, the Ad Hoc Committee chair.[37] Smith opened by urging Chandler to follow the lead of Nickerson, who had appeared before the committee on the previous day, and answer questions he had refused to respond to with HUAC. Smith added, "We certainly do not have in mind at this stage taking for granted any assertions of fact made to us by the Clardy investigator or anybody else, which are undocumented and unsubstantiated as of this stage." Reminding him that the allegations existed, and that the committee ultimately would have to make determinations, Smith left it up to Chandler how to proceed. The hearing then entered the first of what would be two phases.

During the initial phase, Chandler attempted to move the inquiry along the lines he had proposed in his memo. He acknowledged that his refusal to answer certain questions from HUAC left "false impressions" that he wanted to "clear up." He began with a major focus from the hearing, *Operation Mind*.

> The Clardy Committee asked me a series of questions with regard to my activity which they alleged in the Ann Arbor Council of the Arts, Sciences, and Professions. If the answers to their questions had been yes, or even only if every time they said to me, "Isn't it a fact that—," it had been a fact, the facts would have been damaging. . . . And I want to tell you such facts about it as are pertinent to this charge.[38]

Chandler went on to explain that the Council, which no longer existed, had consisted almost entirely of graduate students and faculty from the university. The research and drafting of *Operation Mind* were carried out by two other members. As treasurer of the organization, he signed the check for the production of the pamphlet. Chandler pointed out that the basis for the HUAC questions included two incorrect suppositions. These were the setting of an organizational meeting and that he was the author. The strength of Chandler's argument may have been weakened by the fact that the notes from the Ad Hoc Committee meeting with Appell alleged only that Chandler was responsible for the printing. As mentioned earlier, at the HUAC hearing, members had gone beyond the evidence with their questions, in itself an important point, but one that Chandler lacked the information to make.

Smith asked for other examples of HUAC misinformation. Chandler's response, with the compelling details of the Eisler story, received no reaction from the Ad Hoc Committee. They had already been apprised by the Executive Committee of the College of Literature, Science, and the Arts. Smith inquired if there were still more items. Chandler, whose cache was limited by the questions asked at the HUAC hearing, resisted, hoping to steer the discussion to implications about his integrity that had arisen from the allegation of CPUSA membership. Unable to elicit any response in this vein from the committee, he suggested a possible concern, political relations with students:

> I do feel free and I will insist on retaining the right to discuss politics with anybody I want, including students. I have discussed politics, for instance, with my wife, with older graduate students in my department, with occasional undergraduates, particularly when they took the initiative, and when I was sure that they were people with sufficient maturity to discuss politics with me as an equal. . . .
>
> Now, as for classes, with regard to solicitation of membership, I don't believe I have ever taken the initiative in soliciting membership in a political organization from a student. I cannot be sure of that, because of the fact that I was treasurer of the ASP, and I have been active in other organizations in which it is possible that that might have happened and I can't be sure.
>
> In any event, I can assure you that if it did happen, there was not any form of undue pressure put upon the student.[39]

Chandler had raised and addressed the canard about indoctrination of students by Communist professors. The discussion moved to the definition of a political organization and then the matter of political objectives. Finally, Smith initiated the sort of exchange that Chandler had been trying to generate since the beginning of the hearing:

> CHAIRMAN SMITH: As I gather, you feel that there are certain situations in which the use of violence to achieve political ends can be justified?
>
> DR. DAVIS: Definitely. The first example I would give is where the violence already exists and there is not much you can do to stop it. Normally my primary concern would be to avoid violence, as I will explain later. As the violence exists and there is nothing you can do to stop it, it may be in some cases better to take sides

than not. This is obvious as it is necessary to get it out of the way.

CHAIRMAN SMITH: How about cases where violence does not yet exist?

DR. DAVIS: In any such case, whether it was domestic or international, I think it would be highly desirable, and I will exert myself to the utmost to avoid a violent settlement of the issues. In case achievement of desirable social ends was prevented by habitual violent repression, it might under certain circumstances be desirable. I think that such an instance is the Revolutionary War, where the Declaration of Independence was issued in spite of the fact that there was no large scale campaign initiated from the other side, simply because the democratic expression of desirable political changes, desirable governmental and social changes, was violently thwarted, and there was the threat of larger scale violence thwarting of the people's will.

I might say in this respect, that the internal situation in the United States, at the present time, is darned near as favorable as it could very well be, for the avoidance of violence in my opinion, because of the fact that at least as regards internal affairs we have a long tradition of allowing people their head. I would anticipate therefore that all desirable political changes in the United States can be achieved by free discussion, and it is my great concern that this should be the case, which in large part motivates my opposition to the type of repression that might reduce the people to violent revolution as the only way of expressing their will.[40]

Chandler had carried out his program of answering questions that pertained to his integrity. In the process, he was more forthcoming than he had been with HUAC. The problem was that his logical argument was wasted on the Ad Hoc Committee and administrators who, nevertheless, believed that membership in the CPUSA was grounds for termination. Smith shifted into the second phase of the hearing by confronting what remained essential issues for his committee:

CHAIRMAN SMITH: Now I hope you will answer these questions, I think you should. In any case I think we have to ask them. I think we might just as well start at the beginning, if you are willing.

The first one I think you have answered: "Do you believe in or advocate the overthrow of our present system of government by force or violence?"

DR. DAVIS: The answer is no, because our present system of government is one which can be modified by other means.

CHAIRMAN SMITH: The second question: "Are you a member of the Communist Party or associated with the Communist Party in any way?"

DR. DAVIS: With that, I think I should assume you have read and understood the preliminary statement which I made. You understand there are reasons to me which are very crucial reasons of principle, I might say more important than my job to me, why I do not want to answer political questions; that I wait to be told, in the expectation I will be, which non-political implications of this question you are concerned about and feel necessary to clear up.

If these include perforce answering that question, then of course I will, because I don't want to impede in any way your verification that I am a man of integrity.

CHAIRMAN SMITH: Let's put it this way: suppose the university is convinced, or that a substantial majority of the faculty of the university or those associated with the university should be convinced, or are convinced that membership in the Communist Party is incompatible with the kind of free thought, free marketing of ideas and so forth, which you yourself seem to espouse, would you then consider it pertinent of the university to ask a staff member whether or not he is a member of the Party?

DR. DAVIS: Such a person would have to believe, a person accepting this would have to believe that I have denied it, since I have denied, or since I have asserted, and I will assert again at as much length as you like, and in as much detail as you like, that I am in favor of the free exchange of ideas; that I am not in favor of forming one's ideas by dictation.

If you believe that membership in the Communist Party ipso facto means believing otherwise, then you will have to conclude I have denied it. I am not willing to comment on it.[41]

The reasoning from Chandler's logical argument, that a person cannot be a Communist if they lack a trait shared by all Communists, fell flat with the Ad Hoc Committee.[42] For some time, Davis and Smith fenced over answering variations of the Communist question, without reaching any resolution. Eventually, Smith moved on to the list of allegations from Appell,[43] beginning with whether in 1950 Davis had formally condemned the Supreme Court decision on the Smith Act prosecutions. Seeing the political nature of the question, Chandler inquired whether all these actions were regarded as improper. Smith replied that together they might be construed as a pattern of Communist behavior. When Davis asked to hear the entire list, Smith enumerated the allegations. Hatcher insisted on a point-by-point response. Chandler declined but went on to say that most of the claims were false. For example, an assertion that he participated in a program with Howard Fast and Paul Robeson was easily debunked. To his knowledge, the two men had never been in town at the same time.

The hearing ended, after three hours, at an impasse over Davis's responsiveness. When the Ad Hoc Committee made its recommendations to President Hatcher, it was in unanimous agreement that Chandler should be dismissed.[44] On Markert and Nickerson, the committee was split with majorities in favor of reinstatement under censure.

The Ad Hoc Committee's justification for firing Chandler was "his conduct to date, and particularly his failure to be candid with the representatives of the University concerning his past or present affiliation, if any, with the Communist Party." The committee rejected Chandler's argument that he should be examined only on the questions of integrity others associated with CPUSA membership. In its view, the combination of his refusal to cooperate with HUAC and the allegations of Communist activity by government investigators made it imperative for him to provide straightforward answers to the Ad Hoc Committee. With Chandler's unwillingness to do so, it became "highly probable that he is using his professed principles as a means of avoiding full and candid disclosure of Communist affiliation." The committee believed that "he has artfully contrived to preclude inquiry of him and thus patently lacks the integrity he claims to possess."

To bolster the contention that Chandler was acting in "bad faith," the Ad Hoc Committee offered in its report, from his testimony before them, five alleged "examples of a display of deviousness, artfulness, and indirection hardly to be expected of a University colleague."[45] One of these was a transcript excerpt, similar to the one quoted above, in which Chandler made a logical argument to Smith that the information he sought on integrity could be obtained without the Communist question. In view of the earlier character references of his mathematics colleagues, Chandler's sincerity should not have been so easily discounted.

Another excerpt with supposed indirection was Chandler's deliberately vague responses to questions about the size of the Council of Arts, Sciences, and Professions. Probably the Ad Hoc Committee did not appreciate the difficulty of trying to discern, instantaneously, whether the unanticipated question was of a political nature. What is unconscionable is that their report does not reveal that later in the session, upon appreciating its pertinence to his integrity, Chandler did provide a satisfactory estimate of fifty.[46] The other three examples, when understood in full context, also do not make a case for evasiveness.

Conversely, Markert's and Nickerson's forthrightness about their CPUSA backgrounds, along with the absence of recent activity, satisfied a majority of the Ad Hoc Committee. The committee's doubts arose from the professors' refusal to recant

RecANT!

earlier beliefs. According to historian Ellen Schrecker, the problem for Nickerson and Markert "stemmed from the flawed, but common, assumption that it was not possible to be an ex-Communist without becoming an anti-Communist."[7] Three of the five Ad Hoc Committee members voted to lift both of their suspensions, with the representative from the Medical School supporting Markert and opposing his colleague, Nickerson. The censures were for lack of candor with HUAC.

President Hatcher did not rubber stamp the recommendations of the Ad Hoc Committee that he had gone outside the bylaws to create. He accepted the advice of the committee to reinstate Markert but rejected their similar assessment of Nickerson. On Davis, Hatcher agreed with the committee on termination. Whether he applied the same basis for the decision as the committee was unclear as can be seen in this relevant portion of his letter to Chandler:

On May 10, 1954, you were interrogated under oath by representatives of the House Committee on Un-American Activities which alleged, and whose representative has stated to us, that it possessed information concerning your membership in and associations with the activities of the Communist Party. You were asked by this duly constituted legal body questions as to your past and present affiliations with Communism, whether or not you were a member of the Party while at Harvard University, whether or not you were associated with certain active Communists, whether the State Department revoked your passport because you were a Communist, whether you are now a member of the Communist Party, whether you have solicited members for the Communist Party at Ann Arbor and questions of similar import.

You refused to answer these questions in public testimony on the grounds that this Committee had no right to ask them.

You have taken the same attitude and have refused to answer these or related questions or to talk candidly about yourself and your alleged activities in the Communist Party before me, and the

Special Senate Committee to advise the President, on your own personal decision that the answers are none of our business.

This conduct is inexcusable in a member of our profession who seeks at the same time the protection of and continued membership in the University whose policies he disdains and whose responsibilities he ignores.

Your conduct to date is clearly inimical to the mission and trust reposed in this University, and indicates your unfitness to continue in the position you hold.

In view of the evidence available to me, and of the unanimous recommendation of the Special Committee to Advise the President, I regret to state that it will be my duty to recommend to the Regents your immediate dismissal from the staff of the University.[48]

The Hatcher letter lacked the "reasonable particularity" on the grounds for dismissal to which Chandler was entitled under the bylaws. Discernment of the president's grounds can only be conjectural. Undoubtedly, he believed in the AAU statement and was acting in what he felt was the best interests of the university. In his report to the faculty Hatcher prefaced reproduction of his letter to Chandler with the comment that "[t]he line of questioning by the House Committee on Un-American Activities indicated a rather close and continuing involvement in the Communist apparatus on the part of Dr. Davis."[49] The justification for his decision, in the last paragraph quoted above, indicates he was relying on "evidence available to me, and the unanimous recommendation of the Special Committee [Ad Hoc Committee]." The AAUP Report notes the absence of the reasons provided by the Ad Hoc Committee and states: "We find inescapable the inference that Dr. Davis was dismissed because it was believed he was a member of the Communist Party, and that present membership necessarily involved acceptance of illegal and immoral 'principles and methods.'"[50]

The AAUP Report goes on to furnish two explanations by which Communist Party membership would be an inadequate justification for dismissing Davis. The allegation was unsupported by substantial evidence in the actual record. Moreover, in the AAUP's view, even if it were established, merely "innocent membership" is an insufficient ground.

President Hatcher's reasons for dismissing Nickerson were even less scrutable to the AAUP committee than those for Davis.[51] The president's July 27 letter to Nickerson refers to it being "difficult to accept your disavowal of the illegal and destructive aims of the Communist Party" and the recommendation by the dean and Executive Committee of the Medical School.[52] On the former point, the AAUP Report found the case of Nickerson to be "indistinguishable" from that of Markert, who was reinstated.[53] Out of their investigation, the AAUP committee determined that the grounds of the Medical School administration were inadequate for dismissal.

Records from Markert's FBI files offer insight into President Hatcher's agenda. On July 29, the Director of University Relations informed the Detroit FBI office that the university intended to retain Markert for just one additional year, ceasing his employment at the end of his current contract.[54] Since Markert had successfully undergone a promotion review, the motivation behind his termination must have been his HUAC case. Understanding Hatcher's intention to purge all three faculty members from the university provides an explanation for his dubious Markert-Nickerson distinction. Firing a tenured professor could be difficult. With the backing of the Medical School, Hatcher would dispose of Nickerson on grounds of integrity, while tossing a bone to the liberals by appearing to keep Markert. When the heat died down, a more routine dismissal of Markert might even go unnoticed.

Under Section 5.101 of the Bylaws, the faculty were permitted five days to request a hearing before the bylaw Committee (Subcommittee on Intellectual Freedom and Integrity). Markert chose not to contest his censure sanction. Davis and Nickerson sought review of the recommendations for their termination. The AAUP Report found the handling of these cases by the university to be "seriously prejudiced" in various respects.[55] We focus on the treatment of Davis.

When his five-day clock began on July 27, Chandler's only document from the hearings was the letter from President Hatcher with the vague reasons for his dismissal. Transcripts of the Ad Hoc Committee meetings with the Executive Committees of his college and department existed but were not provided to him, nor was he even given a transcript of his own hearing. Chandler could only infer the allegations, by the government investigators, from questions asked of him by the Ad Hoc Committee. He received the report of the Ad Hoc Committee just a few hours before his hearing with the Bylaw Committee, leaving inadequate time to prepare a defense. The AAUP Report cited these violations of the due process provisions in the Bylaws.

In a "Dear Colleague" statement on July 31, Chandler included another reason for his refusal to answer political questions, coining a term: the "doctrine of compulsory self-labeling."[56] People were forced to place themselves on a continuum between left and right, with those too far to the left being punished. The consequences were a hollowing out of the left by intimidation, with the acceptability point gradually moving rightward.

The case then went to the Bylaw Committee, which the AAUP Report severely criticized for misconstruing its mission. Rather than reviewing the recommendation of the president as intended in Section 5.101, the Bylaw Committee acted as an appellate body for the charges by the Ad Hoc Committee. Thus the Bylaw Committee considered accusations that were no longer central to the proceedings. As it was Hatcher who was proposing dismissal to the Regents, it was his justification that required examination.

Accompanying Chandler at the Bylaw Committee hearing were his department chair, Hildebrandt, and two supportive mathematics colleagues, Wilfred Kaplan and William LeVeque. Participation in the discussion was more widely distributed than it had been at the Ad Hoc Committee meeting. The principal dynamic, however, remained the same. The committee pressed for an answer to the Communist question from Chandler, who adamantly attempted to deflect to the implications about his integrity.[57]

Whether Chandler was a member of the CPUSA was not considered by the Bylaw Committee, which, nonetheless, stated its view on the pertinence of the issue to academic fitness:

> There is evidence that whatever the Party may have been in the past, it is now composed in some significant part of dedicated conspirators. There is also substantial evidence that present membership in the Party carries with it, as its usual concomitant, secret domination by the Party. Such a group, and such a secret domination, go beyond political beliefs, and go beyond the scope of academic freedom. Except in extraordinary circumstances, we would regard present membership in the Communist Party, with its doctrinaire Party domination, as an act disqualifying one from the role of university professor.[58]

The Bylaw Committee went on to affirm that the need of the University to determine if one of its professors was a current CPUSA member trumped Chandler's principle of free speech. They concluded that "the dismissal of Dr. Davis from the university faculty is warranted."[59] Moreover, the Bylaw Committee agreed with the Ad Hoc Committee that Chandler's testimony had been evasive and devious "to a point which reflects upon his integrity."[60] Significantly, both hearing panels were on record believing that Chandler had undertaken an elaborate First Amendment scheme in attempting to deceive them. Usage of the word "devious" in the committee reports was particularly damaging as it played into a second Red Scare trope of Communists. Without any dissent, the Bylaw Committee's recommendations to terminate Chandler and to reinstate Nickerson went to Hatcher. The president urged the Regents to fire both men and to retain just Markert, under censure. The Regents approved what could be viewed as a politically savvy move by Hatcher. He was being tougher than the faculty committees, but appearing to show some mercy, which, as FBI records reveal, was disingenuous.

The ousters of Davis and Nickerson took place late in August. The absence of any severance payments, especially for an action at the very end of the academic year, was deemed as unjust in the AAUP Report.[61] The AAUP censured the University of Michigan in 1958 for its handling of the Davis and Nickerson cases.[62] After changes to the University Bylaws, the sanction was lifted the following year.

The Ad Hoc and Bylaw Committees were wrong in concluding that Chandler was employing the First Amendment in a devious fashion to avoid answering their questions. Likewise, Hatcher was mistaken if he was acting under the belief that Chandler was a current member of the CPUSA. Despite these serious misconceptions, Chandler's days at Michigan would have been numbered even if his circumstances were fully understood. He had been a member of the CPUSA while at the university, and his reasons for leaving the Party did not include a rejection of its ideology. The committees may or may not have been satisfied by forthright responses along these lines, but Hatcher would not, and it was his judgment that was decisive. An irony was that the university was punishing Chandler for belonging to an organization which it regarded as an existential threat and from which he withdrew because it was ineffectual.

The ramifications for University of Michigan personnel from the HUAC subpoenas extended beyond the 1954 summer hearings. Within a week of the termination decisions, President Hatcher received a confidential request from H. H. Saunderson, president of the University of Manitoba. Nickerson was a candidate for a position at the Canadian school. Informed by press accounts of his suspension by Michigan, Saunderson inquired "whether Professor Nickerson has been an active Communist or whether there has been any indication of disloyalty to your government."[63]

While Nickerson's best scenario was a return to his position at Michigan, albeit as *persona non grata* in his department, he had pursued a contingency plan of obtaining a new position. Because his superb scholarly credentials were nullified in a country where CPUSA-priors were toxic, Nickerson looked north of the border to continue his work, in a country where there was some shelter from the second Red Scare. Manitoba, in turn, saw an opportunity to secure a pharmacologist whose attainments rated a more prestigious posting. In his carefully worded response, Hatcher reported on Nickerson's testimony while utilizing a lifeline offered by Saunderson that the behavior could be attributed to stubbornness rather than disloyalty. Hatcher even suggested that in a new environment "it is quite possible that Dr. Nickerson, whose professional status is of the highest, might go forward as a socially more mature citizen."[64]

Nickerson moved to Manitoba, where his pharmacological research did indeed bring distinction to his new home. A decade later, he relocated to McGill University in Montreal and continued to advance his discipline in Canada. Nickerson's contributions were recognized in 1975 with his election to the presidency of the American Society for Pharmacology and Experimental Therapeutics.

Some questions remain about the HUAC effect on Markert's ensuing career at Michigan. Hatcher's plan to discharge him the following year did not materialize. In an interview many years later, Markert recalled going to Dean Odegaard, following his reinstatement, to discuss his prospects at the end of the year remaining on his contract. Markert stated that the dean provided assurance that no dismissal would take place at that time.[65] He later learned that Hatcher refused to approve a department recommendation for continuance. Markert then reached out to Dean Odegaard, whom he subsequently heard had intervened on his behalf with Hatcher. In any event, Markert did receive a second year on the faculty after the HUAC hearings.[66]

Markert made the most of his time at Michigan, convincing his colleagues of his value as a scholar and teacher. Though it is unclear what communication took place between Hatcher and the zoology department during this period, review letters from outside authorities attested to Markert's standing at the top of embryologists of his generation.[67] In 1956, he was promoted to the rank of associate professor with tenure, despite some lingering concern over the issues raised by the HUAC hearing. According to Ellen Schrecker, Markert was the only untenured faculty member in the country to be promoted after defying a congressional investigating committee.[68]

During the review process, the zoology department became aware that Johns Hopkins and the University of Chicago were exploring the possibility of bringing Markert to their institutions.[69] At least Hopkins requested a statement from Hatcher that would clear Markert of any remaining questions over his status.[70] Niehuss obliged with a report on Markert's promotion and excellent prospects for further advancement.[71] Markert eventually accepted a full professorship from Johns Hopkins. The record does not reveal any effort by Michigan to respond with a counteroffer. In 1965, Markert was called to Yale to become chair of the Department of Biology. Two years later, he was inducted into the National Academy of Sciences.

Markert's award of tenure at Michigan is all the more remarkable when considered in light of the treatment of Lawrence Klein at about the same time. Recall that Klein had voluntarily informed the university of his CPUSA past. He followed the AAU guidance in cooperating with HUAC, even receiving the approbation of Clardy. Unlike Davis, Markert, and Nickerson, Klein was neither suspended nor reviewed for possible discipline.

At Michigan, Klein was then leading a groundbreaking

project to produce a macroeconometric model for the United States economy.[72] With Klein abroad at Oxford University for the 1954–55 academic year and his HUAC hearing seemingly in the past, the new Michigan economics chair, Gardner Ackley, decided the time was ripe to press for Klein's promotion to professor.[73] To support the unusual advancement, Ackley solicited evaluations of Klein's research and standing from leading authorities on econometrics. His choice of five international scholars was admirable.

Among this group were Jan Tinbergen and Ragnar Frisch who would be the recipients of the Nobel Prize in Economics when it was first awarded in 1969. Completing the list of referees were subsequent Nobel laureates Wassily Leontief and Tjalling Koopmans and the then current chair of the President's Council of Economic Advisors, Arthur Burns. Although Frisch did not immediately reply, the other four provided strong support by expressing enthusiasm for Klein's work. Leontief placed him on a short list of the foremost American scholars in quantitative economics that included future Nobel Prize winners Robert Solow and James Tobin. Koopmans opined that "I honestly think that your attempt to bring Dr. Klein back to this country has national importance for improved knowledge of our economy." It was stunning that the thirty-four-year-old Klein had attracted the attention and praise of such a distinguished collection of authorities.

When the Department of Economics faculty met to consider the promotion case, William Paton expressed vehement opposition. He believed the professorship was unwarranted, challenged the need for development in econometrics, and condemned Klein's past Communist activity and current socialist beliefs. Paton was a pioneering figure in the study of accounting who carried considerable influence within the university and among its alumni. A longtime professor in the School of Business Administration, Paton held a joint appointment in economics where he did not teach. His own political views were far-right and strongly held. The vote of the economics faculty was 18–2 in Klein's favor with Paton joined in opposition by a colleague from the School of Business Administration.

Consideration of the promotion moved to Dean Odegaard and the Executive Committee of the College of Literature, Science, and the Arts. Odegaard permitted Paton to elaborate on his opposition arguments, which were conveyed to Ackley for rebuttal. In a move of dubious fairness to Klein, Odegaard solicited new evaluations from ten economists proposed by Paton. Likely out of an effort toward evenhandedness, Odegaard requested appraisals from five additional names provided by Ackley.

Once again Ackley's list, all of whom solidly endorsed Klein, included four future Nobel Prize winners. The responses from Paton's nominees were mixed, including support and criticism. As pointed out by Ackley, none of Paton's ten possessed expertise in econometrics, and only half were distinguished scholars.[74] Moreover, some had axes to grind, such as bias against Keynesian economics and a grievance over an unfavorable reference to him in a review by Klein.

Odegaard and the Executive Committee considered the arguments and voted unanimously to support Klein's promotion.[75] It remained for Niehuss and Hatcher to determine whether to present the case for approval by the Regents. Their decision was to compromise, forwarding a recommendation to promote Klein to a professorship, but without the tenure that was approved by the Department and Executive Committee.[76] Instead, Klein would be recognized as a staff member of the Institute for Social Research, carrying an expectation for annual reappointment. Tenure could be awarded at a future time.

Naturally, Klein was disappointed.[77] He liked Michigan but was anxious to settle somewhere with his family. Uncertain what to infer about his future prospects in Ann Arbor, Klein began to consider other offers he was receiving. In June, the Regents approved the untenured professorship. After Ackley allayed his concerns, Klein agreed to return to Michigan.

Paton, who had been rebuffed on an extraordinary request to make his arguments against Klein directly to the Regents, brooded over what he regarded as an outrageous promotion.[78] Venting to Niehuss, Paton urged that the appointment be limited to a single year. Breeching protocol, he carbon-copied five Regents on the letter. The primary effect of Paton's interference was to cause considerable aggravation for Niehuss and Hatcher. The administrators did, however, check with the FBI to satisfy themselves that Klein's record was clean in Ann Arbor.[79]

Amidst the earlier uncertainty over his appointment, Klein had arranged for an additional term at Oxford during the fall of 1955. He carried on his work in England, blissfully unaware of Paton's scheming, until a bizarre missive prompted him to reconsider his future plans. Writing to Ackley on October 18, Klein began: "A few weeks ago, I received an anonymous letter outlining Paton's recent moves against my appointment."[80]

The phantom writer went on to accurately depict Paton's approaches to the Regents and to reveal a threat of his widening the nasty campaign against Klein to the general public. Ackley asked Niehuss to reassure Klein of his status at Michigan. Whereas Ackley's earlier letters had made tenure appear certain in the near future, Niehuss was more circumspect. He suggested that Klein should be able to continue as a lecturer if the recommendation for continuance of his untenured professorship were not approved the following year.[81] Klein decided to accept a long-term position created for him at Oxford.[82]

A few years later, Klein returned to the United States to join the faculty at the University of Pennsylvania, remaining there until retirement. In 1980, he was awarded the Nobel Prize in Economics "for the creation of econometric models and their application to the analysis of economic fluctuations and economic policies." Had Klein received tenure in 1955, it is likely that the University of Michigan would have shared in his acclaim. President Hatcher's failure to advance Klein's stellar case through the Regents was a blunder in University stewardship of historic magnitude.

The motivation behind Paton's attacks on Klein is less certain. Undoubtedly, the passionate anti-Communism of the second Red Scare was a major factor. Historian David Hollinger has pointed to evidence that anti-Semitism underlaid Paton's animus.[83] In her 1979 research for a history of the Michigan economics department, Marjorie Brazer's faculty interviews included some discussion of the Klein incident.[84] William Haber recalled having "sensed" an "anti-Semitic overtone" in Paton's references to Klein, including to a sound in his voice that was often associated with Jewish people. Gardner Ackley was more explicit in his allegation of anti-Semitism. Ackley remembered Paton telling him that the appointment of Klein was part of a "plot . . . to solidify Jewish control of the department." It should be pointed out that Ackley's recollections in 1979 were somewhat faulty, raising the possibility that he was conflating various conversations with Paton. In the view of this author, the Brazer materials are insufficient to go further than to raise the possibility that anti-Semitism was behind Paton's actions.

The equanimity with which Gardner Ackley treated Klein's political beliefs did not extend to the two economics graduate students who pleaded the Fifth Amendment at the HUAC hearing. Ackley had information, confirmed by the administration, that Edward Shaffer and Myron Sharpe were members of the CPUSA.[85] Whereas Hatcher suspended the three faculty members immediately following the hearing, he took a week to consider the disciplinary consequences of the uncooperative testimony by Shaffer and Sharpe.

The headline in the May 19 *Michigan Daily* was NO CHARGES AGAINST STUDENTS. A statement from Hatcher explained that students were under less severe obligations than those for faculty. However, should Shaffer and Sharpe be found in contempt of Congress, as Clardy had suggested in Lansing was possible, they might then face a hearing on their conduct before a university committee. Academic sanctions were left in the hands of the economics department and the graduate school.

When news of Hatcher's decision reached Clardy, the congressman conveyed his disappointment to the president in a letter.[86] Clardy confirmed his intention to pursue contempt charges against the graduate students, but he explained that the process was complex and that it may not succeed. He wanted Hatcher to know his personal opinion that Sharpe and Shaffer were unworthy of "further honor" from his alma mater. Clardy did not mention that the Fifth Amendment assertion left little basis for a contempt charge beyond Sharpe's belligerent behavior at the hearing. Clardy's initiative to urge expulsion of the students was indicative of HUAC's modus operandi of relying on outside bodies to impose punishment on unfriendly witnesses.

The question of academic consequences arose in the fall when the economics department recommended that Sharpe be admitted to candidacy for a PhD. In light of the recent HUAC hearings and at the behest of the graduate school, the department agreed to reconsider whether Sharpe and Shaffer were qualified for the candidacy standing that was essential for advancement to a degree. Ackley oversaw the review by the economics faculty. His six-page, single-spaced report on the department's determinations included disparaging assessments of both students, followed by a dubious disclaimer:

> First of all, it should hardly be necessary to state that none of us has the faintest sympathy for the apparent political and social convictions of these students. We believe that their behavior outside of the classroom—for example before the Clardy Committee—may well be regarded as reprehensible. We suspect them of insincerity and anti-democratic attitudes. . . .
>
> Our failure to admire or like these men is, however, irrelevant.[87]

Ackley went on to write that the department found no academic basis, even when considered in a broad sense, for a denial of candidacy. Sharpe and Shaffer were entitled to an opportunity to complete their degrees by producing satisfactory theses. The seemingly principled stand was then belied by an outright admission that the economics faculty would engage in the blacklisting that was afflicting the academy.[88]

> We freely confess that individually we could not, and will not, recommend either of these men for teaching or research positions. It has been urged that, if we cannot recommend them, we should not grant the degree. But there is a great difference between a private letter of recommendation, giving a personal evaluation, and the formal, legal act of recording course grades and granting degrees. In our hiring, in our personal and private associations of every kind, we may consider impressions of character, political beliefs, perhaps even religious views.

Ackley's duplicitous position may have been sincerely held, but evidence indicates that his economics colleagues, by their actions, ignored the magnanimous aspect of the memo. For while both Sharpe and Shaffer went on to successful careers in the field of economics, neither received a PhD from Michigan. Sharpe recalled his dealings with his advisor, Harold Levinson: "Each time I handed him a draft of my thesis he changed his requirements. Finally, after three years of following his instructions, I was asked to redo the whole thing."[89] Sharpe abandoned the degree, eventually becoming an innovative publisher in the social sciences.[90]

By itself, Sharpe's thesis experience possibly could be explained by unrealistic expectations of his own or by a single biased member of the economics faculty. But consider his dissertation experience together with that of Shaffer.[91] Fired from two part-time jobs and in dire financial straits after the HUAC hearing, Shaffer left graduate school and found employment in New York. Eight years later, leveraging his experience with an oil consulting firm, he sent a dissertation proposal, concerning a recently established export program, to his advisor at Michigan. The response from the Director of Graduate Studies was discouraging. The Graduate Committee found the dissertation proposal to be a shallow combination of well-known facts and obvious conclusions. Not only would Shaffer need a much more substantial proposal to continue on his degree, but another year of residence and retaking the preliminary exams that he previously had passed.

Skeptical that his case was being handled objectively, Shaffer sought a second opinion from a Columbia University economist. Examination of the same dissertation proposal led to his admission to Columbia with a fellowship. Three years later Shaffer received his PhD, and his thesis was published in book form. In 1988, he retired as professor of economics from the University of Alberta.

Sharpe and Shaffer only learned of Ackley's letter when informed by the author forty years later. The covert blacklisting of Michigan left-wing students went beyond economics. Steve Smale applied for faculty positions in mathematics as he was completing his thesis in 1956. Nothing materialized at first. Then Smale had the good fortune to be advised by a benevolent professor to discontinue using his department chair, Hildebrandt, as a reference.[92] The other professor was visiting Princeton where he learned that Hildebrandt included the remark "quite active in a liberal student group" in his recommendation of Smale. Although the characterization understated Smale's actual political involvement, the coded phrase was sufficient to disqualify him from jobs in 1956. Smale managed to obtain a position elsewhere. He soon began obtaining outstanding results that attracted international attention. In 1966, Smale received the Fields Medal, often referred to as the Nobel Prize of mathematics.

The effectiveness of HUAC's campaign against the left

wing on university campuses owed much to the enabling of administrators and faculty. Of the five faculty and two graduate students subpoenaed at the University of Michigan, only Chandler Davis was indicted. It was university personnel that fired Nickerson and Davis, overrode tenure recommendations for Klein and Markert, obstructed degrees for Shaffer and Sharpe, and essentially sabotaged the employment prospects of Smale, Shaffer, and Sharpe. Although Smale was not sufficiently prominent then to draw the attention of HUAC, his antiwar work and notoriety as a mathematician would lead to a HUAC subpoena in 1966. In his case, a University of California at Berkeley administrator and the director of the National Science Foundation conspired to hold up Smale's research funding from the government agency.[93]

Felix Frankfurter and Earl Warren, 1955.

CHAPTER EIGHT

The Path to the Supreme Court and the Frankfurter Effect

Early in 1954, Chandler decided to undertake a First Amendment challenge to the legality of the HUAC hearings. The most recent ruling on the issue had been the 1949 Court of Appeals for the District of Columbia Circuit decision against the Hollywood Ten. This unanimous opinion, concluding that the Communist question was within the purview of HUAC, was controlling in the DC Circuit, but still subject to review by the Supreme Court. Chandler's case was in the Sixth Circuit.

Predicting future Supreme Court decisions is hazardous, particularly as the makeup of the Court may change during the period that a case winds through the District Court and the Court of Appeals. Beyond the First Amendment stalwarts Hugo Black and William Douglas, no member of the 1953–54 Supreme Court possessed a record aligned with Chandler's position. Though Chief Justice Earl Warren would later become known for charting the direction of a liberal court, he was then its newest member, and in his first year. Having previously served as a prosecutor and most recently as governor of California, Warren was just developing his judicial philosophy.[1]

Justice Felix Frankfurter, despite his earlier notoriety as a liberal Harvard professor, had become an advocate of judicial restraint and thus, for reasons that will be explained shortly, disposed against reining in Congress. Tom Clark was the attorney general who had brought the original Smith Act indictments. The remaining justices were Robert Jackson, Stanley Reed, Harold Burton, and Sherman Minton, whose conservative sympathies were likely to favor HUAC over the CPUSA. It was difficult to conceive of a majority for Chandler's case out of the current bench or any replacements likely to be selected by Republican President Dwight Eisenhower.

In the fall of 1954, Chandler faced more pressing concerns than the makeup of the Supreme Court. He was without an income or an attorney. As a short-term measure, a very pregnant Natalie took on a campus clerical job. Chandler flooded the United States academic market with applications, only to find that he was persona non grata amid the second Red Scare.

Yet Chandler and Natalie were gratified by the support they received from many individuals. A local fund drive on their behalf by department colleagues netted over $2,000.[2] Chandler speculated that his prominent reference, Paul Halmos, "wrote more letters for me than anybody had ever written for anybody before," all to no avail.[3] To circumvent the blacklist, Chandler would need to abandon, at least temporarily, a career he loved.

By this time, Chandler had experienced some success as an author of science-fiction stories. As with members of the Hollywood Ten, he considered pursuing a living as a writer under an assumed name but decided against it. Chandler could not get beyond his self-image as a mathematician for whom science fiction was a sideline.[4] A more lucrative opportunity soon arose, however, that could serve as a stopgap.

Through a mutual friend, Chandler was acquainted with

another First Amendment HUAC defendant, Lloyd Barenblatt (discussed in chapter 6). Barenblatt had obtained a position with an advertising firm in Manhattan that was unaware of his criminal case proceeding through the courts. In 1955, following a tip from Barenblatt, Chandler began doing market research for another advertising company on Madison Avenue.[5] Secrecy about his indictment was essential to maintaining the arrangement.

Obtaining an attorney remained problematic for Chandler. After failing to consummate arrangements with Ann Fagan Ginger and William Robert Ming, Chandler turned to Corliss Lamont, chair of the Emergency Civil Liberties Committee. From a family of considerable wealth, Lamont himself had received subpoenas and contempt citations from both HUAC and McCarthy's Senate Subcommittee on Investigations. Lamont agreed that his committee would cover Chandler's legal expenses and connected him to his own attorney, Philip Wittenberg.

Wittenberg would represent both Chandler and Barenblatt in their 1956 federal district court trials. Chandler was tried in Grand Rapids, Michigan, where he faced an indictment for refusing to answer questions in the HUAC hearing. The judge was W. Wallace Kent, and the prosecutor was U.S. Attorney for the Western District of Michigan Wendell Miles, both appointees of President Eisenhower.[6]

In preparing the case against Chandler, Miles sought assistance from the FBI.[7] Of particular interest to him was intelligence that might be helpful in setting up a perjury charge if Chandler were to testify. The FBI regarded Chandler as a "bad actor" whose conviction was a priority. The discussion of what could be provided to Miles, without compromising sources or operations, went to a high level. During this review, Chandler was added to Hoover's secret COMSAB (Communists with a potential for sabotage)[8] and DETCOM (Communists to be detained in the event of war with the Soviet Union) lists. The FBI drafted memoranda for Miles with information from their files about Davis and Wittenberg.

The FBI then undertook consideration of whether to provide Miles access to an informant who would testify that Chandler was a member of the CPUSA. The issue was always sensitive because testimony typically marked the end of an operative's usefulness in obtaining information. A few months earlier a possible solution arose. Sydney James, a graduate student in history at Harvard, then provided information to the FBI.[9] As a Harvard undergraduate in the late 1940s, James had been a member of the CPUSA. Under pressure from his dean, McGeorge Bundy, James disclosed a substantial number of Communists from his Party days. The list included Chandler, who was a graduate student at the time. Since James was unlikely to obtain any future intelligence, there would be no downside for the FBI to his testimony.

When approached by the FBI, James was reluctant to testify about Chandler.[10] He already felt guilt over his complicity with investigators. Moreover, his information was hearsay and of dubious value in court. James declined to cooperate. The remaining option was Irving Rozian, the Ann Arbor engineer from the Council on Arts, Sciences, and Professions. The FBI concluded that Rozian's continuing value as an informant outweighed whatever contribution he could make to Chandler's prosecution.[11]

Chandler was charged with 26 counts of violating Title 2, United States Code, Section 192. Each count involved refusal to answer a particular question from the subcommittee. The actual statement of the law included:

Every person who having been summoned as a witness by the authority of either House of Congress to give testimony or to produce papers upon any matter under inquiry before either House, or any joint committee established by a joint or concurrent resolution of the two Houses of Congress, or any committee of either House of Congress, willfully makes default, or who, having appeared, refuses to answer any question pertinent to the question under inquiry, shall be deemed guilty of a misdemeanor, punishable by a fine of not more than $1,000 nor less than $100 and imprisonment in a common jail for not less than one month nor more than twelve months.

It was indisputable that Chandler had been summoned to give testimony by HUAC and that he had refused to answer their questions. Whether the inquiry was appropriate and the questions "pertinent" left room for argument. Not only were there constitutional issues, but there were also procedural matters that could be challenged. Wittenberg was an experienced attorney, familiar with recent court developments, who was ready to make every argument on his client's behalf.

On February 2, 1956, Judge Kent conducted a hearing on a motion to dismiss Chandler's indictment.[12] Wittenberg went over the indictment count by count, identifying what he claimed were fatal defects. For example, prior Supreme Court rulings restricted congressional investigations to areas where the committee was permitted to legislate. Because *Operation Mind*, with its criticisms of HUAC, enjoyed the protection of the First Amendment, he said the several inquiries about the pamphlet were outside the reach of Congress.

Other questions, Wittenberg argued, failed to meet the "pertinence" requirement of the statute. In addition, referencing prior cases at various levels, he alleged that the congressional committee was attempting to expose unpopular views and associations in order to subject Chandler to public scorn. Such harassment constituted usurpation of the punishment function reserved for the judiciary and was thus in violation of the constitutional separation of powers.

On a more mundane level, Wittenberg challenged the indictment as defective on due process grounds. Just five of the questions were followed by a directive to answer. None of the counts included the allegation that there was a "willful" failure to respond. Wittenberg claimed that, under recent rulings, these flaws were fatal errors necessitating dismissal of the corresponding counts.

In rebuttal, Miles chose other cases to argue that every count of the indictment was sound. He emphasized that each of the subcommittee's questions was aimed at "getting information for the purpose of aiding in the passing of legislation."[13] If it happened that any of these legitimate questions might lead to self-incrimination then the defendant was free to exercise his Fifth Amendment right, of which he was apprised and declined to avail himself.

Miles stated that, from the transcript, Chandler had made clear after the question in the first count that he understood the circumstances and that further direction was unnecessary. Judge Kent accepted this argument as well as the language in the indictment stating that the defendant "deliberately and intentionally refused to answer" as a satisfactory substitution for "willful."[14] He determined that questions concerning pertinence should be resolved at trial.

Judge Kent concluded that Congress had the "the right to investigate the influence of Communism in the educational institutions of this country." He noted that recent legislative matters pertained to educational institutions at all levels. Kent ruled that the indictment was satisfactory, rejecting Wittenberg's motion to dismiss.

Wittenberg probably did not expect to win on any of the challenges. Instead, he wanted to accumulate a record for appeal. For his part, Chandler was uncomfortable with all the procedural contentions. He was anxious to make a First Amendment appeal to the Supreme Court. Having the case dismissed on a technicality at the district level would thwart these plans. Chandler conveyed his concerns to Wittenberg, who "patiently explained that for him to fail to raise all possible technicalities would be falling short of professional standards and make the courts not take him seriously."[15] While attorney and client interacted amicably, they were not, nor would they become, simpatico over how to conduct the defense.

The trial took place in November 1956.[16] Chandler declined a jury trial since "acquittal by a jury would have no consequences for future cases."[17] For the prosecution, Miles relied on congressional documents and transcripts and just two witnesses, HUAC counsel Frank Tavenner and subcommittee chair Kit Clardy. The thrust of Miles's argument was that the questions asked of Chandler were both for the purpose of preparing congressional legislation and pertinent to an investigation of Communism in education.

The counts in the indictment ranged over several areas: Communist activity at Harvard and Michigan, *Operation Mind*, and Chandler's passport revocation. Miles claimed that the questions were motivated by a desire to obtain information related to actual legislation being contemplated or, in some cases, proposed by HUAC. In his examination of Tavenner and Clardy, Miles elicited testimony that the HUAC agenda included modifying the Smith Act to make CPUSA membership a crime, and to withhold federal support from educational institutions that permit faculty to advocate Communism. On passports, HUAC had recommended additional questions in the application to ascertain whether the trip itinerary included Iron Curtain countries. Clardy proudly asserted that his own legislation to deny second-class postage for distribution of un-American propaganda was inspired by *Operation Mind*.

Miles argued that all the questions arose out of information in the possession of HUAC. Prior witnesses had revealed the existence of communist cells at Harvard and Michigan, institutions where Chandler had studied and taught. From the State Department, the Committee knew that Chandler's passport had been confiscated. From another source, they were aware that Chandler had ordered the printing of *Operation Mind*. No claim was made that Chandler was a member of the CPUSA, probably because of the FBI's unwillingness to provide an informant. Thus, Miles argued that the Communist question was legitimized by the Barsky court decision.

Wittenberg, who did not call any witnesses, objected early and often. He claimed that testimony from previous hearings was inadmissible due to the absence of its confirmation and a lack of opportunity for cross-examination by him. Wittenberg pointed out that consideration of legislation by HUAC did not imply its constitutionality. He alleged that the entire Lansing hearing was a failed political stunt to enhance Clardy's prospects for reelection. In the end, Wittenberg appealed to the judge to see reasonable doubt of pertinence and legislative purpose.

In his decision Judge Kent reiterated that "Congress is entitled to all information relating to any Communist activities of the teaching personnel in the universities and colleges of this country in determining the propriety of any proposed legislation."[18] On the pertinence contention, Kent ruled that "the questions which form the basis for the Indictment in issue were directed toward a determination not only of the attitude of the defendant toward Communists and Communism, but also as to the activities of other persons who may or may not have been involved in Communist activities in institutions other than the University of Michigan. To say that such inquiry is not pertinent to the subject of the investigation is to ignore the realities of the situation."

Kent found Chandler guilty on all counts. He explained that probation was an inappropriate penalty because, faced again with the same circumstances, Chandler was likely to repeat the same criminal behavior.[19] The sentence was a $250 fine and six months in jail.

Chandler's legal case became linked with those of John Watkins and Lloyd Barenblatt, both of whom declined to answer questions in contemporaneous HUAC hearings. They were found guilty of contempt in district court trials preceding Chandler's.

THE PATH TO THE SUPREME COURT

Appeals in the *Watkins* case were interlaced with the district court proceedings for Chandler.

CHRONOLOGY OF WATKINS APPEALS AND DAVIS DISTRICT COURT DEVELOPMENTS

JANUARY 26:	Watkins Appeals Court decision
FEBRUARY 2:	Davis District Court hearing
APRIL 23:	Watkins Appeals Court (en banc) decision
NOVEMBER 19:	Davis District Court trial
JUNE 17:	Watkins Supreme Court decision
JUNE 25:	Davis District Court decision

That the *Watkins* case was reviewed and decided by the Supreme Court had considerable ramifications for both Chandler and Barenblatt. For example, the seven-month interval between Chandler's trial and Kent's decision is explainable by a wait for the Supreme Court's decision on *Watkins*. That the controlling rulings and their ruminations in the *Watkins* appeal decisions shifted at each level presented special challenges to Wittenberg and Miles in making their arguments. The notion of pertinence was a decisive consideration throughout.

Recall that Watkins responded to all questions from HUAC about his own CPUSA background. He refused to answer questions concerning CPUSA membership by past associates whose current status he was uncertain of. Rather than citing the Bill of Rights, Watkins asserted that such questions were beyond the authority of HUAC. Representing Watkins was civil rights attorney Joseph Rauh, whose other HUAC defense clients included writers Lillian Hellman and Arthur Miller.[20]

Watkins was fortunate that his Appellate Court panel included Henry Edgerton who had written the minority opinion in the *Barsky* case. Judge David Bazelon joined Edgerton in the majority for the 2–1 January verdict to overturn the

District Court conviction of Watkins. The reasoning relied on the purpose behind the questions that Watkins refused to answer.

Edgerton framed the case as follows: "If the questions Watkins would not answer were pertinent to the inquiry authorized by the Act [creating HUAC], we should have to decide whether they were within the constitutional power of Congress." He went on to say that while Congress has the power "to investigate matters and conditions relating to contemplated legislation . . . It cannot be used to inquire into private affairs unrelated to a valid legislative purpose."

Much of the discussion involved the issue of "exposure":

It is very questionable whether exposure of individuals to public contempt or hostility is a "valid legislative purpose." Since Congress has "no powers of law enforcement" it would have no power, in the absence of a valid legislative purpose, to expose former Communists, even if there were a law requiring that former Communists be exposed. If we were obliged to decide what the Committee's purpose was in asking the questions Watkins would not answer, we might be forced to conclude that the Committee asked them for the sole purpose of exposure.

By "exposure" we mean injurious publicity. privacy

The government contended that the purpose behind the questions in contention was the investigation of Communist infiltration into labor unions. HUAC was considering legislation to deprive Communist-dominated unions from access to the National Labor Relations Board. The Edgerton opinion observed that the particular questions asked were to confirm whether individuals, already named by others, were members of the CPUSA a decade earlier. Watkins had responded about some but not others. For the people he had responded about, there was no follow-up about their influence. "The Committee showed no interest in anything but a list of names." Moreover, in the dynamic world of labor organization, the judges asserted that dated information was of little value for current legislation.

Edgerton quoted from his minority opinion in *Barsky*: "The committee and its members have repeatedly said in terms or in effect that its main purpose is to do by exposure and publicity what it believes may not be done validly by legislation." To support this statement, he supplied numerous quotes from past committee chairs and their reports.

After making the case that the evidence pointed to the committee's purpose being one of "exposure," the majority found: "In our opinion the questions that Watkins refused to answer are not pertinent to the inquiry authorized by the Act. . . . We conclude that the government failed to show, either beyond a reasonable doubt or even by a preponderance of the evidence, that the questions Watkins would not answer were pertinent to any investigation the committee was authorized to make." Finally, they argued that the opinion was not in conflict with either *Barsky* or *Lawson*. In particular, *Lawson* pertained to motion pictures, which fell under the propaganda dissemination authority of the committee.

HUAC chair Francis Walters was outraged by the ruling. He asked a House Appropriations Subcommittee to investigate the backgrounds of Edgerton and Bazelon.[21] Rather than appeal directly to the Supreme Court, the government requested, and was granted, a rehearing en banc (that is, before the entire Court of Appeals for the District of Columbia Circuit). In April, with just Edgerton and Bazelon dissenting, the Court of Appeals reinstated Watkins's conviction.[22] Majority and minority opinions from the panel flipped with Judge Walter Bastian now speaking for the Court:

> A majority of the court is of the opinion that Congress has power
> to investigate the history of the Communist Party and to ask the
> questions Watkins refused to answer. It would be quite in order
> for Congress to authorize a Committee to investigate the rate of

growth or decline of the Communist Party, and so its numerical strength at various times, as part of an inquiry into the extent of the menace it poses and the legislative means that may be appropriate for dealing with that menace. Inquiry whether thirty persons were Communists between 1942 and 1947 would be pertinent to such an investigation.

Bastian went on to state that *Barsky* addressed the First Amendment objections raised by the defense over the particular questions. As to the allegations of exposure: "Congress has power of exposure if the exposure is incident to the exercise of the legislative function." Clearly there was a disagreement among the judges over whether the exposure was peripheral or central to the hearings.

The reversal in opinions from the panel to en banc led to an awkward moment for Wittenberg. In the February district court hearing, Wittenberg's presentation incorporated elements from Edgerton's (then) majority opinion. When Miles quoted from Bastian's (then) minority opinion, Wittenberg interjected derisively about the lack of relevance of a dissent to law. In the November district court trial, Miles took especial delight in quoting the first sentence from the portion of Bastian's (then) majority opinion, displayed above.

Despite the fact that Edgerton and Bazelon proved to be outliers on the District of Columbia Circuit, their January panel majority for Watkins provided an indication of the vincibility of HUAC, as well as the remarkable luck of Watkins. One last appeal remained. At the rendering of the en banc decision in April 1956, two years had passed since the 1954 HUAC hearings of Watkins, Davis, and Barenblatt. During this interval, the only personnel change on the Supreme Court was a consequence of the death of Justice Robert Jackson. President Eisenhower appointed John Harlan, another conservative, to replace Jackson. Also of significance was that Warren's transition into a liberal was under way.[23]

According to legal scholar Bernard Schwartz, "The Watkins case graphically illustrates the importance of chance in Supreme Court decisions."[24] Once again Watkins was most fortunate. For between the en banc ruling and commencement of oral argument on March 7, 1957, one-third of the justices withdrew from the case.

1. Harold Burton recused himself because his nephew was a counsel for the government.
2. Sherman Minton retired on October 15, 1956.
3. Stanley Reed retired on February 25, 1957.

Schwartz was "virtually certain" that each of these three justices would have voted to uphold the conviction of Watkins. The seating of the replacements was equally impactful. William Brennan, who to Eisenhower's dismay would become a liberal icon, joined the Court on the day after Minton's retirement. Charles Whittaker, who as a district judge dismissed Chandler's father's suit against the University of Kansas City, was seated two weeks after the Watkins Supreme Court hearing. The overall effect was the conversion of three votes against Watkins into one vote in favor, and a four-person liberal majority (Black, Douglas, Warren, and Brennan) among the seven judges deciding the case. Prior to describing the arguments and adjudication, a digression is needed to provide some background on Frankfurter and Warren, who would have crucial roles in the outcome.

Frankfurter was a prominent and enormously influential person, even prior to his tenure on the Supreme Court.[25] In 1894, at the age of eleven, Frankfurter emigrated with his family from Austria to the United States. He graduated from City College of New York and then distinguished himself as a student at Harvard Law School. After a brief stint in private practice, Frankfurter entered public service as an assistant to the United States Attorney for the Southern District of

New York, Henry Stimson. When Stimson was appointed
Secretary of War, Frankfurter continued his apprenticeship in
Washington. There the young attorney argued cases before
the Supreme Court[26] and began influential relationships with
Louis Brandeis and Oliver Wendell Holmes.[27]

In 1914, Frankfurter became the first Jewish professor at
Harvard Law School. In addition to taking on teaching duties,
he fashioned a role as a public intellectual. Frankfurter was one
of the principals in launching the progressive periodical *The New
Republic*. When Louis Brandeis joined the Supreme Court in
1916, Frankfurter took over some of his advocacy for labor
reform and other social welfare causes. Chapter 3 in this book
touched on Frankfurter's campaign for due process after the
Palmer Raids. Later he attained considerable notoriety for his
work on behalf of the anarchists Sacco and Vanzetti during
their prosecutions.

The Supreme Court fascinated Frankfurter, who closely
studied its rulings, culture, and history. He cherished his inti-
mate connection to Brandeis and Holmes, sending the best
Harvard law graduates to serve as their clerks. During the 1920s,
Frankfurter was appalled by the activism of a conservative Court
majority, which overturned labor laws promulgated to protect
workers against abuse. Not only were these rulings offensive
to his progressive ideals, but they violated the judicial philosophy that Frankfurter had been formulating over the years. Legal
scholar Melvin Urofsky describes the general governing principle
Frankfurter adopted, inspired by the writings of James Bradley
Thayer at the end of the nineteenth century:

> For Frankfurter, the answer to the crisis could be found in
> judicial restraint and institutional deference. The legislatures
> represent the majoritarian will, and courts should not second-
> guess the wisdom of their policies. Unless a statute violates a
> clear constitutional prohibition, courts should not void a law
> because judges disagree with its premises.[28]

After Franklin Roosevelt became president, judicial restraint was the basis for Frankfurter's criticism of the Supreme Court's annulment of crucial planks from the New Deal. When Roosevelt finally got the opportunity to replace justices in the late 1930s, his first nominees were Black, Reed, Frankfurter, Douglas, and Frank Murphy. Many observers expected Frankfurter to lead the Roosevelt bloc into a new era of liberal rulings. They were mistaken.[29] Despite his intense study of the Court, Frankfurter's temperament and judicial philosophy eroded his influence and left him with a legacy that is at best mixed.

In a chapter titled "The Failure of Leadership," Urofsky begins with Frankfurter's incapacity to treat his judicial brethren as peers:

> For 30 years, however, Frankfurter had been either an aco-
> lyte to men he recognized as great figures—Holmes, Brandeis,
> Stimson, and Roosevelt—or a preceptor and mentor to those he
> considered his intellectual inferiors; the master-disciple rela-
> tionship was not going to work with those who saw themselves
> as his equals and were not beholden to him for their positions
> on the nation's highest court. One of the great tragedies of
> Frankfurter's career is that a man renowned for his talents in
> personal relations, who knew so well the high value justices
> placed on careful collegiality, could so terribly misread the
> situation and the characters of those with whom he served.[30]

Urofsky goes on to document Frankfurter's arrogance, insults, and condescension in legal discussions with the justices. Sometimes the disparagement was direct, and at others expressed to a third party about a colleague. Neither was endearing. In recent years, Court watchers marveled over how, despite their antipodal views, Ruth Bader Ginsburg and Antonin Scalia maintained a congenial relationship. Frankfurter personalized disagreement, accumulating his resentment in a tab. Already by 1943 he was referring to Black, Douglas, and Murphy as the Axis.[31] Further examples of the internecine struggles among the Roosevelt appointees are provided by current Harvard Law professor Noah Feldman in his book *Scorpions*.[32]

Thus, rather than gaining support through persuasion as was characteristic of the affable William Brennan, Frankfurter's exhortations were alienating. According to Urofsky and Feldman, however, the primary reason behind Frankfurter's failure to live up to expectations as a justice was the straitjacket he placed himself in with his strict adherence to the doctrine of judicial restraint. As the court docket shifted from issues of property rights to those of civil liberties during the second Red Scare, Frankfurter continued his deference to the legislature. He would not adjust his judicial philosophy to the new circumstances.

> It is not that Frankfurter lacked a vision, but rather that time outran his vision; he would have been the perfect judge a generation earlier. Once on the bench he seemed ignorant of the tides of history, of the country's changing social and political climate—the same sins for which he as an academic commentator had lambasted the conservative judges of the 1920s and 1930s. He remained consistent, but consistency is not always a virtue.[33]

A consequence of Frankfurter's rigid devotion to judicial restraint was becoming identified with the side of forces with which he was in conflict. When Frankfurter adopted the restraint philosophy, his Court positions aligned him with the social welfare movement that he supported on behalf of labor. Applying the same legislative deference dogma during the second Red Scare associated him with the purveyors of McCarthyism. Frankfurter detested the tactics of HUAC, characterizing the Committee as consisting of "loose-mouthed, loose-mannered and loose-headed men."[34] Yet he endured the unwelcome baggage, probably accepting the criticism as the plight of a great judge.

In contrast to Frankfurter's doctrinal framework, Earl Warren approached decision-making from the perspective of "ethical imperatives" embodied in the Constitution.[35] Prior to his appointment as Chief Justice, Warren served as district attorney for Alameda County and then attorney general and governor of California. As governor, he was a progressive and nonpartisan Republican with a reputation for accomplishment. Depending on the issue, Warren could be regarded as conservative or liberal. For example, he was adamantly anti-Communist, but he advocated for a state role in guaranteeing health insurance.

Powerfully influencing Warren were his youthful observations while working for the Southern Pacific Railroad. The company regularly exploited its employees, who lacked any avenue for recourse.[36] Warren became empathetic with hard-working people oppressed by overwhelming forces. One fundamental theme of his subsequent judicial philosophy was described as "identification of the language in the Bill of Rights with protection of the natural rights of man against the arbitrary actions of government."[37]

In October 1953, Warren assumed leadership of a Supreme Court that included the legendary justices Hugo Black, William Douglas, Felix Frankfurter, and Robert Jackson.[38] Confident in his abilities, but wise enough to exercise humility, Warren was initially cautious in asserting his authority. For the first few conferences, he asked Black, the senior justice, to lead the case discussions. Warren was also solicitous of advice from his colleagues. Frankfurter interpreted the overtures as an opportunity to cultivate the rookie justice.

Through the first two years of Warren's tenure as Chief Justice, the overriding issue for the Court was the historic *Brown v. Board of Education* case. Frankfurter and Warren were allies in what remains a widely praised unanimous decision to overturn the practice of segregated education. Their exchange of notes during this period, generous with advice from Frankfurter, were reciprocally welcomed.[39]

When the *Watkins* case reached the Supreme Court, Warren was completing his fourth year as Chief Justice. In his oral argument for the appellant, Joseph Rauh emphasized two points.[40] First, that as a "corollary to the separation of powers," the congressional "power to investigate does not encompass exposure unrelated to a legislative purpose." And second, that "the purpose of the Committee here in interrogating petitioner was to expose him and his former associates to scorn and ridicule."

Much later in his presentation, Rauh made a stipulation that raised the First Amendment: assume that there was some legislative purpose to exposure, which he did not concede. "Legislative purpose is not legislative need. You still must balance the repressive effects of the activities of the Committee on speech and association against the need for the legislation."

During his rebuttal, Solicitor General J. Lee Rankin insisted that the inquiry of Watkins was not motivated by exposure. Rather, it was part of an investigation into CPUSA infiltration of unions, which led to legislation a few months later. As to the First Amendment issues, Rankin asserted they were unrelated to Watkins, but to the people about whom he was being asked. Moreover, the First Amendment addressed the right to speak, not the right not to speak.

Frankfurter interrupted the presentation of Rankin to ask whether, when Watkins declined to answer, the chair had explained the pertinence of the question. It was a point to which Frankfurter returned repeatedly, eventually obtaining a concession from the Solicitor General that the chair had merely directed Watkins to answer the question.

Watkins was among the cases considered by the justices at a conference on the next day. By tradition, in these discussions the Chief Justice expresses his views first and is followed by the other justices in order of decreasing seniority. Each includes their judgment, subject to future change, on whether to affirm or reverse the decision under review. Then the Chief Justice, if in the majority, designates a member of this group to draft the opinion for the Court. Otherwise, the authorship selection is made by the senior member from the majority.

Justices Harold Burton and William Douglas recorded notes on the *Watkins* discussion.[41] Warren spoke favorably of Watkins's good faith effort to cooperate with the subcommittee, sympathetic to his drawing the line at becoming an informer. The Chief Justice gave two reasons for reversal. First was the failure of the subcommittee to justify the relevance to Watkins of the questions to which he was unresponsive. Also troubling Warren was HUAC's abuse of its power in exposing an individual's private behavior to advance the committee's legislative agenda.

Frankfurter, consistent with his stance in oral argument, agreed that there was a burden on the subcommittee to establish relevancy. But following his philosophy of judicial restraint, he stressed that the basis for the ruling should be narrow, leaving congressional committees broad investigating power. All of the justices, except Clark, advocated overturning Watkins's conviction. Among Harlan's papers is a note dated March 9, 1957, supporting Frankfurter's position: "Only ground for reversal I can see is that Watkins was entitled to a clearer explanation as to the relevancy of the questions. And I need more study for this. [I don't see how we can say this is 'exposure' or not within Committee authority.]"[42]

Warren designated himself to write the *Watkins* opinion. On May 21 he circulated a first draft of his argument for dismissing the indictment.[43] After describing the facts in the case, Warren gave a detailed history of contempt prosecutions in Parliament and the Congress. The last portion was a ruling on the failure to inform Watkins of the pertinence of the questions. In the middle of his draft, Warren confronted the Freedom of

Speech issue in HUAC testimony that the Supreme Court had evaded, to this point, by passing up the *Barsky, Josephson,* and *Lawson* cases:

> There can be no doubt that the investigative process is capable of resulting in abridgment of First Amendment freedoms. Whenever a witness is compelled, against his will, to reveal his beliefs, expressions or associations, his right to engage in such conduct free from governmental interference has been impinged upon. And when those forced revelations concern matters that are unorthodox, unpopular or even hateful to the general public, the reaction in the life of the witness may be disastrous. This effect is even more severe when it is past beliefs, expressions or associations that are exposed in light of the changing conditions in political affairs. Nor does the witness alone suffer the consequences. Persons who are identified by others and placed in the same glare of publicity are subjected to public stigma, scorn and obloquy. Beyond that there is the more subtle and unmeasurable effect upon those who tend to adhere in the future to the most orthodox and uncontroversial views and associations in order to avoid a similar fate. That this impact is partly the result of non-governmental activity by private persons cannot relieve the investigators of their responsibility for initiating the reaction.
>
> Translating the strictures of the First Amendment into a practical rule for determining the proper bounds of a congressional investigation is as arduous a task today as it was when *United States v. Rumely* was before the Court. We do not underestimate the difficulties that attend such an undertaking. Despite the adverse effect that follows upon compelled disclosure of matters protected by the First Amendment, we cannot hold that all such inquiries are barred. Where the force of the impact is slight or speculative, and public need for availability of such information to the Congress is great, presumably the individual interest in privacy must give way. However, we

cannot simply assume that every congressional investigation that results in abridgment of First Amendment freedoms is justified by a public need that overbalances any private rights affected. To do so would be to abdicate the responsibility placed by the Constitution upon the judiciary to ensure that the Congress does not encroach upon rights protected by the First Amendment.

Petitioner has earnestly suggested that the difficult questions of application of the First Amendment to legislative inquiries can be surmounted in this case because there was no public purpose served in his interrogation. His conclusion is based upon the thesis that the Subcommittee was engaged in a program of exposure for the sake of exposure. The sole purpose of the inquiry, he contends, was to bring down upon himself, and others, the violence of public reaction because of their past beliefs, expressions and associations. In support of this argument, petitioner has marshalled an impressive array of evidence that some Congressmen have believed that such was their duty, or part of it.

We have no doubt that there is no congressional power to expose for the sake of exposure. Whatever may be the function of Congress to inform the electorate on matters of the conduct of the government, there is no power to expose where the effect is to abridge First Amendment liberties of private citizens. But such a rule does not afford a solution to our problem. It would require delving into the motives of Congressmen in a proceeding to which they are not parties. Their motives, moreover, would not vitiate an investigation that had been authorized by a House of Congress if that assembly's purpose is being served. If a committee is actually carrying out its mandate, the personal motives of the members seem immaterial.

In further examination of the problem, Warren placed the blame on an excessively vague authorizing resolution that made it impossible to determine that the HUAC subcommittee's invasive actions were justifiable. All told, the discussion of the compelled testimony aspect of the case occupied about 10 of 34 pages.

Douglas replied swiftly to Warren with his approval of the draft.[44] Although not insisting, Douglas suggested for consideration that the discussion excerpted above be predicated upon separation of powers, as had been argued by Rauh, rather than the First Amendment. Among Harlan's papers is an edited copy of the first draft that includes deletions of most of the First Amendment material. It seems unlikely that Harlan conveyed these revisions to Warren, as there is no surviving correspondence, and his specific language was not implemented.

In contrast, Frankfurter, who shared the view of Harlan, memorialized his communication with the Chief Justice. In a three-page letter, Frankfurter attempted to present his criticism in a positive light by stating: "*Watkins* is not a First Amendment case as the emphasis of your opinion overwhelmingly demonstrates."[45] Nevertheless, Frankfurter made clear that he was raising an issue of importance to him. "This is by no means a technical point . . . I deem the foregoing vital lest witnesses before a congressional committee parrot-like repeat the phrase, 'First Amendment, First Amendment, First Amendment.' We get into a lot of trouble by talking about the plain and unequivocal language of the First Amendment in its provision about 'abridging the freedom of speech.'"

Under the principle of judicial restraint, Frankfurter believed the courts should defer to the legislature, regardless of their unseemly practices, as long as they followed due process. Frankfurter made comments and "concrete" suggestions to Warren on the draft.[46] He annotated the previously excerpted paragraphs with separate marginal remarks: "Watkins refusals were not based on the First Amendment and we do not have to adjudicate that the bearing of First Amendment to Congressional inquiries is," "This on its face is not a First Amendment case," and "Some of us may not find an infringement of the First Amendment." Frankfurter's specific revisions attempted to cleanse the term "First Amendment." For example, he suggested replacing "in abridgment of First Amendment freedoms" with "in indefensible abridgment of protected freedoms" and substituting "protecting these rights from infringement by" for "application of the First Amendment to."

Although Frankfurter and Warren agreed on reversing the decision based on the subcommittee's failure to establish pertinence, the justices had a fundamental conflict over whether HUAC was in violation of the Bill of Rights in their treatment of Watkins and Barenblatt. In his second draft on May 29,[47] Warren made the revisions requested by Frankfurter. Though it is doubtful that these local changes to the ten pages would have made the opinion palatable to Frankfurter, Warren added an additional paragraph to the end of the compelled-speech discussion. In the original draft, this portion lacked any conclusion as to whether or not the questioning of Watkins was permissible. In the second version, Warren inserted the following paragraph with an explicit ruling:

> We conclude that the questioning of petitioner by this committee, through the means of compulsory process, cannot be approved. That body has been established as an independent investigative subsidiary of the House of Representatives with virtually no guidance or control by the full House. It is thus impossible to ascertain whether any legislative purpose justifies the disclosures sought from petitioner and, if so, the importance of that information to Congress in furtherance of its legislative function. Since the House itself has never made this determination, no court could reasonably do so. Lacking this knowledge, it is, of course, impossible to accommodate the public interest involved in the disclosures the Committee demanded from petitioner with whatever may be the private

rights affected. The conviction of petitioner, therefore, must be reversed.

This paragraph, had it survived to the final opinion, could have had enormous ramifications for Davis, Barenblatt, and others. Judge Kent was waiting for the *Watkins* decision to make his ruling on Chandler. It is difficult to see how a Supreme Court holding invalidating the interrogation of Watkins would not carry over to Davis as well as to Barenblatt whose case was awaiting appeal.

Needless to say, the second draft failed to mollify Frankfurter. He had been speaking with Harlan and knew that they held similar views on the case. Frankfurter proposed further modifications to Warren, including deletion of the new paragraph, restoring ambiguity on the civil liberties issues.[48] He closed his cover letter with this statement: "It is in the spirit in which I have written this letter that the concrete suggestions herewith have been made and with the eager anticipation on my part that your final product will be such as to enable both me and John to join your opinion unreservedly."[49] On the same day, Harlan informed Warren that he was "ready to join in your opinion on *Watkins*" while adding that he still hoped that "the decision" could be rested "solely on your second ground."[50]

Frankfurter was placing pressure on Warren with the not so veiled threat, somewhat undercut by Harlan, to reduce his majority from six to a weaker four plus two concurrences. Moreover, he led Warren to believe that, with the changes, he would sign on to the opinion. Warren implemented all of Frankfurter's revisions, including elimination of the recently added paragraph.[51] Harlan quickly notified Warren of his intention to join,[52] as did Frankfurter, thanking the Chief Justice "for the consideration you have given to my suggestions."[53]

Within two days Frankfurter reneged, drafting a concurrence

to clarify the aspects of Warren's opinion with which he was in agreement. For the *Watkins* decision announced on June 17, 1957, the vote was five for Warren's opinion plus the Frankfurter concurrence, with only Clark in dissent.[54] Amazingly, it was Frankfurter who felt he was the aggrieved party on *Watkins*, venting in a letter to Learned Hand two weeks later about Harlan and Warren, after first impugning "the present 'hard-core' 'liberal wing' of the Court."

Their common-denominator is a self-willed, self-righteous power lust, conditioned by different causes, internal and external, undisciplined by adequate professional learning and culti-vated understanding.

And John, with all his judicial aims and character, really has not had the appropriate intellectual background of reading and reflection for the ultimate task, that of passing on consti-tutionality. He makes me wince when he talks about questions being "in the First Amendment area" and having "an instinct" that this or that "power of Congress is extremely limited"— limited that is, by the goulash of narrow-minded prejudices of Earl, & Black & Douglas & Douglas,[55] their prejudices & their respective pasts & self-conscious desires to join Thomas Paine & T. Jefferson in the Valhalla of "Liberty" and in the meantime to have the avant garde of the Yale L. School & the Edmond Cahns praise them! Moreover, he is not meant for battle, represents at its best what I'm told is the dominant Princeton ideal, to be "nice," and is just the kind of person who is too ready to have a bully like Black & a "martinet" (the word is John's) like Warren have their way. You will have a good example of what is in my mind when I tell you—between ourselves—that he tried hard to persuade not to file the con-curring opinion in the Watkins. It was a sufficient weakness on my part even to join qualifiedly—by way of interpretation of its holding—Warren's much and excessive & poor rhetoric (by way of a woolly-headed law clerk), but John urged me not to publish. Why? "You may only stir up rancor" was his reply. To which I, "John, you can always have what is called peace if you yield to the bullies & the irrationalists. I don't mean to be extravagant, but because of such yielding to Hitler the world is now where it is." When he went off the other day I put a copy of J. B. Thayer's essay in 7 Harv. L. Rev. into his hands, with the remark "Please read it, then re-read it, and then read it again & then think about it long."[56]

Frankfurter's disrespect for the other justices is stunning. Even Harlan, his ally, was treated as a student in need of remedial guidance.

Beyond his arrogance, Frankfurter's bad faith was an intolerable machination among the brethren who were constantly struggling over consensus. One year later Warren reached his breaking point when another late concurrence from Frankfurter betrayed his commitment to join a unanimous ruling in the *Cooper v. Aaron* case.[57] Thereafter, "Warren regarded Frankfurter as his antagonist."

For John Watkins, the contempt of Congress prosecution was over after three years. Warren's controlling opinion dwelled on dubious practices by HUAC in its handling of investigations and stated, "There is no congressional power to expose for the sake of exposure." Frankfurter, however, had weakened the First Amendment discussion and removed the holding that the interrogations were impermissible. The only explicit ruling was on the narrow due process issue of establishing pertinence to the witness.

In its June 17 session that unveiled the *Watkins* decision, the Supreme Court announced findings in three other Communist-related cases. A companion state-level case, *Sweezy v. New Hampshire*, overturned the conviction of Paul Sweezy, who was investigated following a guest lecture at the University of New Hampshire. While denying he was a CPUSA member, Sweezy refused to answer certain political questions from the state attorney general about himself and others. *Yates v. United States* became an unsuccessful prosecution under the Smith Act that freed five California CPUSA leaders and raised the bar for conviction under the law.[58] Finally, *Service v. Dulles* ruled that a foreign service officer was improperly fired after being accused of having Communist ties.[59]

What were universally viewed as defeats for McCarthyism were major stories in the press.[60] On the following day the front-page headline in the *New York Times* was HIGH COURT, RELEASING WATKINS, RESTRICTS CONGRESS ON PRIVACY; FREES 5 REDS IN SMITH ACT CASE, accompanied by three articles on the Court rulings.[61] In his piece, James Reston wrote: "The Supreme Court today warned all branches of the Government that they must be more faithful to the Constitutional guarantees of individual freedoms. Reasserting its ancient role as a defender of the Constitution and the Bill of Rights, the high court condemned the tendency to punish men for beliefs and associations, warned the Federal Executive to guard the constitutional freedoms of its employees, and sharply criticized the Congress for giving undefined and unlimited powers of investigation to Congressional Committees." Elsewhere, on *Watkins*, conservative columnist David Lawrence lamented, "the court has opened the way to Communists, traitors, disloyal citizens and crooks of all kinds—in business and in labor—to refuse to answer any questions which the witness arbitrarily decides for himself are not 'pertinent' to a legislative purpose."[62]

The tone of Warren's *Watkins* opinion, together with the other verdicts that day, led many observers to overestimate the effect. Lawrence grumbled that HUAC "might as well close up shop." Liberal pundit I. F. Stone predicted that "June 17, 1957, will go down in the history books as the day on which the Supreme Court irreparably crippled the witch hunt."[63] McCarthy had died a month earlier, but vestiges of McCarthyism were still alive.

The immediate impact of *Watkins* on other cases was mixed. One week later, Judge Kent found that "nothing in that opinion [*Watkins*] can be construed in such a manner as to change the conclusion that the court has reached" in the Davis conviction.[64] Kent went on to rule that the pertinence issues were satisfactorily addressed.

A few days after the finding against Chandler, the District of Columbia Circuit decided that *Watkins* was determinative on *Singer v. US*, one of several cases that the Supreme Court remanded to their circuit for reconsideration in view of *Watkins*. Marcus Singer was a Cornell biology professor who had refused to name names in a HUAC hearing. In a two-sentence *per curiam* ruling citing *Watkins*, a panel that included Edgerton[65] unanimously overturned Singer's contempt conviction.[66]

Meanwhile, HUAC continued their hearings. Early in 1958 former Party member Ed Yellin was subpoenaed to testify at a HUAC hearing. After reading the *Watkins* decision, Yellin concluded that invocation of the First Amendment was a satisfactory basis for refusing to answer questions.[67] He was indicted six months after the hearing.[68]

While *Yates* effectively ended the prosecution of CPUSA members under the Smith Act,[69] the applicability of *Watkins* to other contempt cases was judge dependent. The Supreme Court still had not ruled explicitly on whether the First Amendment shielded HUAC witnesses from the Communist question, leaving Chandler Davis and Lloyd Barenblatt to continue to pursue appeals through the courts. The Barenblatt case, which was similar to that of Chandler, was further along in the process.

The District of Columbia Circuit heard Barenblatt's appeal several months before the Supreme Court took up *Watkins*. Barenblatt had the misfortune to appear before a panel that included Bastian, but not Edgerton. The unanimous decision upheld his conviction, reaffirming *Barsky*. Barenblatt appealed to the Supreme Court. His case, as with Singer's, was among those returned to the Circuit Court after *Watkins*.

For its reconsideration of *Barenblatt* on October 27, 1957, the District of Columbia Circuit met en banc. David Scribner represented Barenblatt, who had parted ways with Wittenberg after his district court trial.[70] To Edgerton, the appropriate disposition was obvious. Relative to *Watkins*, he saw the case as equivalent to *Singer* that had already been reversed. Affirmation would violate a precedent of the Court from a few months earlier.

The brief decision in *Singer* did not elucidate the case's connection to *Watkins*. In his opinion on *Barenblatt*, Edgerton provided greater detail. A crucial element was the vagueness of the HUAC authorizing resolution that was criticized in *Watkins*. Edgerton wrote: "I understand *Watkins* to hold that the Committee on Un-American Activities had no authority to compel testimony because it had no definite assignment from Congress. The Supreme Court said: 'When First Amendment rights are threatened, the designation of power to the Committee must be clearly revealed in its charter.'"[71]

In another opinion on *Barenblatt*, Bastian adopted the position that it was only necessary to review the pertinency considerations. Note that Frankfurter's paragraph deletion from the second draft of Warren's opinion was critical to making this formulation possible. Bastian asserted that "[t]he *Watkins* situation is a far cry from that of *Barenblatt*." In particular, he claimed that statements by the committee counsel along with the questions asked of Barenblatt and his accuser, Crowley, made clear the nature of the proceeding. Moreover, "The record of the hearing, at which Barenblatt appeared and during which the questions in controversy were asked, is devoid of any objection interposed on the ground of pertinency."

Edgerton and Bastian presented two different approaches to the task of "consideration in light of *Watkins*." Bastian restricted attention to the only explicit ruling in *Watkins*, whereas Edgerton inferred a ruling from two separate findings. A third opinion, by Judge Fahy, concluded that together *Watkins* and *Sweezy* prohibited HUAC prosecutions for contempt in investigations of education.

The District of Columbia Circuit affirmed Barenblatt's conviction on a 5–4 vote with four other justices joining Bastian, and one each for the opinions by Edgerton and Fahy. Curiously, Bastian received the support of both of the members who, with Edgerton, had overturned the judgment against Singer.[72] It would appear that Edgerton was especially persuasive on the June panel that reviewed *Singer*.

The court victories for Watkins and Singer, and even the close decision on *Barenblatt*, indicated a more favorable judicial climate than had existed when Chandler took up his First Amendment defense four years earlier. In the interim, he remained blacklisted and under FBI scrutiny.

The Davis family moved to Yonkers to facilitate Chandler's employment in Manhattan. His FBI file reveals that the Bureau took the initiative to follow Chandler's relocation and position in the advertising firm but apparently did not inform his employers of the controversy surrounding their employee. Seeing Barenblatt fired after a newspaper article mentioned his case,[73] Chandler appreciated the precariousness of his own job. When an opportunity arose in 1956 for a position teaching mathematics in the Columbia night school, he switched to the lower-paying but more congenial duties.

The academic year 1957–58 provided Chandler with an unusual opportunity to devote himself to mathematics again. First, he was successful in the keen competition for a National Science Foundation Postdoctoral Fellowship. Surprisingly, Congress did not intervene as had occurred several years earlier when an open CPUSA member was awarded an Atomic Energy Commission Fellowship. Second, the prestigious Institute for Advanced Study, dedicated to research at the highest level, agreed to host him in their bucolic Princeton, New Jersey, environs.[74]

At that time, the Institute for Advanced Study consisted of two schools, Mathematics (including theoretical physics) and Historical Studies. World-class scholars comprised the Institute's small permanent faculty. Each year a number of visitors, called members, already with doctoral degrees, completed the campus. In 1957, Chandler was one of ninety-three members in mathematics,[75] provided with ideal conditions and complete freedom to conduct their research.

Chandler differed from the typical member who was on temporary leave from the faculty at a university. He also carried the burden of the slow and inexorable movement of his case. On April 24, 1958, Chandler traveled to Cincinnati for the review by the Court of Appeals for the Sixth Circuit. One of the judges on the panel was future Supreme Court justice Potter Stewart. Wittenberg advanced arguments that had gained traction in other recent cases. Among his contentions were a failure to apprise of pertinency and Edgerton's dissent on *Barenblatt*, as well as various procedural issues. The panel decided to hold their decision in abeyance, waiting for a Supreme Court ruling on *Barenblatt*, which had just been granted certiorari.

Indeed, the cases of Davis and Barenblatt shared crucial elements. Both appellants were former CPUSA members who, based on the First Amendment, had refused to answer any question from HUAC about their connection to Communism. They even held the same Meiklejohn justification. Certainly, their cases were closer to each other than either's was to the ambiguous precedent of *Watkins*.

The problem with *Watkins* was that the opinion of the court, a product of efforts by the ideologically differing Warren and Frankfurter, tiptoed around the central First Amendment issue. In *Barenblatt*, the protagonists, Harlan and Black,[76] would write separately, directly confronting the controversy with different resolutions. Once again, a brief digression will provide some background on the two leading actors, who, though vastly different in background and philosophy, grew to become close friends.

After graduating from Princeton University, John Harlan received his legal education at Oxford while on a Rhodes Scholarship. He then became a leading New York corporate attorney with clients such as Dupont. After a brief stint on the Court of Appeals for the Second Circuit, President Eisenhower appointed Harlan to fill the Supreme Court seat of the recently deceased Robert Jackson.

Harlan's judicial philosophy was described by his biographer, Tinsley Yarbrough, as "the belief that the political processes and the principles of federalism and separation of powers ultimately were more significant safeguards of individual liberty than specific Constitutional guarantees."[77] These views aligned with Frankfurter's judicial restraint. In the rare instances when Harlan sided with the liberals, his rulings tended to be narrow, such as in *Yates* where he stiffened the criterion for conviction but did not overturn the Smith Act.[78]

In contrast to the patrician background of Harlan, Hugo Black was born in a rural Alabama town located near the Georgia border. His law degree was from the University of Alabama. Black settled in Birmingham where he established a prosperous personal injury practice.

In 1926, with the support of the Ku Klux Klan, of which he was a member, Black won election to the United States Senate.[79] As a member of Congress he gained influence while following a liberal, populist agenda. Embracing the New Deal, Black became President Roosevelt's first appointment to the Supreme Court.

From his earliest days on the Court, Black began developing a judicial philosophy known as originalism, specifically that "the text of the Constitution means what it was originally intended to mean."[80] The term *originalism* is more frequently associated with recent justices such as Antonin Scalia, who employed its principles to provide justification for conservative positions such as overturning *Roe v. Wade*.[81]

Black was a voracious reader who intensively studied American history, among many subjects, to ascertain the intent of the Founding Fathers. He came to view the Bill of Rights, and in particular the First Amendment, as sacred text. In a 1952 dissent Black wrote:

> I further believe that the First Amendment grants an absolute right to believe in any governmental system, discuss all governmental affairs, and argue for desired changes in the existing order. This freedom is too dangerous for bad, tyrannical governments to permit. But those who wrote and adopted our First Amendment weighed those dangers against the dangers of censorship, and deliberately chose the First Amendment's unequivocal command that freedom of assembly, petition, speech, and press shall not be abridged.[82]

Independently, Black had reached the same conclusion as Alexander Meiklejohn that all political speech, including advocacy of Communism, was protected by the First Amendment.[83] This was good news for Barenblatt and Davis, as far as it went. For the inclinations of the other justices, review of the deliberations on *Watkins* provides considerable insight as to what to expect on *Barenblatt*.

Although *Watkins* was a 6–1 reversal, both Frankfurter and Harlan decided on narrow grounds and were averse to the First Amendment argument. Assuming they accepted the pertinency analysis of the Bastian Appeals Court majority, the decision on *Barenblatt* was likely to be much closer. The case would be heard by two justices who had not participated in *Watkins*. One of these would be Charles Whittaker, who joined the Court two weeks after the oral argument on *Watkins*.

Today, Whittaker's resumé, like that of Black, would eliminate him from serious consideration for a seat on the Court.

Raised on a farm in Kansas, he dropped out of high school after his mother's death, eventually receiving a degree through evening study at an unaccredited law school.[84] The next three decades of Whittaker's life were the inspiring story of his rising to become a successful attorney and partner in a law firm where he had labored as an office boy to support his prior study.

President Eisenhower, who regarded himself as a Kansan, appointed Whittaker to the District Court and then to the Court of Appeals for the Eighth Circuit. In choosing a replacement for Stanley Reed, one consideration for Eisenhower was his displeasure with Warren. The president resolved to make judicial experience a prerequisite for future appointees.[85] Whittaker became the second judge to serve at all three federal levels.[86]

Other Supreme Court justices, such as Black, had surmounted humble beginnings to achieve notable tenures on the Court. Unfortunately, Whittaker was out of his depth. Most remembered for his indecisiveness, Whittaker, according to Schwartz, "may have been the worst Justice of the century."[87] He was ill-suited to hold a pivotal role in resolving a fundamental question of constitutionality.

Votes on the granting of certiorari offer some indication of a justice's disposition toward a case. Not to hear *Barenblatt* would have finalized his conviction. Black, Brennan, Douglas, and Warren voted for certiorari, providing the required minimum of four. The denials of Clark, Frankfurter, and Harlan were to be expected from their positions on *Watkins*. The opposition of the conservatives Burton and Whittaker was no surprise, but rather a portent of difficulty for Barenblatt should the same personnel be in place to hear his case in the fall of 1958.

Burton, however, was afflicted with Parkinson's disease. He retired at the beginning of the 1958 term. In all likelihood his successor would cast the deciding vote in the conference on *Barenblatt*, and thus settle *Davis* as well. In a diary entry about his exit interview, Burton described Eisenhower's thinking on the appointment.[88] The president was troubled by the liberal rulings of Warren and Brennan. He wanted a conservative this time. The only name that came up was Potter Stewart, who had served on Chandler's appeals court panel.

Stewart, unlike Whittaker, possessed impeccable credentials. His undergraduate and law degrees were with honors from Yale, with a year of postgraduate work in between at Cambridge. Stewart would be Eisenhower's fifth, and last, appointment to the Supreme Court. He would become viewed as a moderate during the Warren years.

For the Supreme Court hearing Barenblatt expanded his legal team. Arguing on his behalf was Edward Ennis, general counsel of the American Civil Liberties Union. Many years later Barenblatt recalled, with some bitterness, how his circumstances changed after being granted certiorari:

> Nobody wanted to be my lawyer when I was tried. By the time my case came up to the Supreme Court ... *everybody* wanted to be my lawyer! So the second appeal was handled by the American Civil Liberties Union, which originally wouldn't touch the case. Where were they when I needed them?[89]

Oral argument on *Barenblatt* took place before the Supreme Court on November 18, 1958.[90] Ennis began by asserting that the conviction should be reversed based on the holding in *Watkins* of the need to apprise the witness of pertinency. Harlan interrupted to ask whether Barenblatt made "any inquiry as to what the purpose of the question was." Ennis, though not conceding that such a request was necessary, suggested an objection was expressed in Barenblatt's reference to the *Jones v. SEC* case in his statement that was placed in the record.

Next Ennis went on to combine the Appeals Court dissents by arguing that its authorizing resolution did not empower HUAC

to investigate Communism in education. To preempt a justification included in the government's brief, he pointed out that
inclusion of the topic in committee reports and congressional
debate over appropriations was no substitute for specific authorizing language.

Ennis's final contention was that the HUAC investigation
was in violation of Barenblatt's First Amendment rights. He
claimed that under the recent ruling in *NAACP v. Alabama*
"disclosure of association of private persons cannot be compelled unless governmental authority justifies that intrusion
into private affairs by an overriding public interest." Relying
upon other decisions, Ennis further suggested that HUAC
was restricted in their investigation of Communism to aspects
that involved "inciting immediate action toward the over-

throw of the government by force or violence." But rather than
subversion, HUAC was investigating Communist thought and
associations, which were protected by the Constitution.

Frankfurter and Stewart pushed back on the right of congressional committees to compel testimony for a proper legislative
purpose. Stewart pointed out that people have a right to study
arithmetic, and asked whether Congress could compel testimony
on how many students were studying arithmetic in connection with a grant of federal funds to an educational institution.
Significantly, Stewart, the likely swing vote, was expressing skepticism over the relevance of the First Amendment.

Philip Monahan delivered the rebuttal. He asserted that, under
Watkins, a witness must object to a lack of pertinency during
the hearing in order to raise the issue at trial. Furthermore, he
declared that Barenblatt had not made such an objection. Black
then pointed out that the subcommittee had refused to allow
Barenblatt to make a statement that included the quotation from
Jones covering the objection. Monahan acknowledged that the
statement did eventually become part of the record, but his
contention that the overall tenor of the long document was in a
different direction did not satisfy Black.

Monahan conceded the vagueness of the authorizing resolution, declaring that it should be understood "with the gloss of a lengthy legislative history which shows clearly that the purpose of the House in setting up the committee was to investigate [fascism] . . . and Communism." As anticipated by Ennis, Monahan went on to say that the exploration of Communism in education was thoroughly discussed during the 1953 debate over the HUAC appropriation.

Turning to the legality, under the First Amendment, of requiring an answer to the Communist question, Monahan launched into a long diatribe against the CPUSA. He concluded that the CPUSA was not a traditional political party where membership carried constitutional protection. Monahan then argued that, with its considerable financial support of education, the government was justified in exploring whether CPUSA members were infiltrating the faculty. As relevant precedents he cited several municipal cases and the lower court rulings in *Barsky* and *Josephson*.

A few days later, the justices discussed their assessments of the case.[91] Although Frankfurter had persuaded Warren to delete much of the First Amendment consideration from his *Watkins* opinion, the Chief Justice had not changed his view on the matter. Perhaps reading the room, Warren, however, decided to push for a reversal on the basis of *Watkins* and an inadequate notice of pertinency. Frankfurter disagreed that there was a due process violation, submitting that Barenblatt received a satisfactory explanation.

The other justices voted along expected lines, leaving a 4–4 tie for the most junior member to break. Stewart sided with Frankfurter, Clark, Harlan, and Whittaker to affirm the conviction. Frankfurter designated Harlan to write the opinion for the majority. In his notes on the case, Harlan broke his analysis into the categories of "authorizing resolution," "purpose of investigation," "questions," and "pertinency," each of which he annotated with "OK." On the Communist question, Harlan emphasized the distinction that Watkins, unlike Barenblatt, was responsive about himself.[92]

Harlan, in his draft circulated on February 10, 1959, sought to clarify three aspects of the holdings of *Watkins*.[93] He declared first that the reversal of the lower court decision was based "solely" on the "ground" that "Watkins had not been adequately apprised of the subject matter of the Subcommittee's investigation or the pertinency thereto of the questions he refused to answer." Second, that while *Watkins* was "critical" of the authorizing resolution, the Court did not "h[o]ld the grant of this power in all circumstances ineffective." And whether the First Amendment protects individuals from responding to the Communist question from HUAC "involves a balancing by the courts" in which "[t]he critical element is the existence of, and the weight to be ascribed to, the interest of the Congress in demanding disclosures from an unwilling witness."

The opinion by Harlan included Monahan's arguments on Barenblatt's lack of objection to grounds of pertinence, as well as the gloss of legislative history on the authorizing resolution and investigation into the field of education. As for the government's interest in obtaining an answer to the Communist question, Harlan built on an axiom of a society's "right of self-preservation." He then referred to "the long and generally accepted view that (the tenets of the Communist Party include the ultimate overthrow of the Government of the United States by force and violence." The bottom line was "though we accept petitioner's contention that compulsory disclosure of an individual's association with unpopular and dissident causes impinges on First Amendment protections ... we nevertheless conclude that in this instance such impingement is overcome by the superior governmental interest."

The members of the majority promptly conveyed their approval of Harlan's draft.[94] Frankfurter patted himself on the back for his judgment in assigning the opinion. Stewart suggested a few modifications, the only one of any significance was to delete the concession that there was any impingement on the First Amendment. Harlan made the changes.[95] The opinion for the Court appeared to be set and simply waiting for the dissent that would be prepared by Black.

For Black when it came to the First Amendment, any balancing was sacrilege. He took umbrage with every aspect of Harlan's balancing test, even arguing that it was a misinterpretation of *Watkins*.[96] What was to become one of Black's most famous passages was the following:

> To apply the Court's balancing test under such circumstances is to read the First Amendment to say "Congress shall pass no law abridging freedom of speech, press, assembly and petition, unless Congress and the Supreme Court reach the joint conclusion that on balance the interests of the Government in stifling these freedoms is greater than the interest of the people in having them exercised." This is closely akin to the notion that neither the First Amendment nor any other provision of the Bill of Rights should be enforced unless the Court believes it is *reasonable* to do so. Not only does this violate the genius of our *written* Constitution, but it runs expressly counter to the injunction to Court and Congress made by Madison when he introduced the Bill of Rights. . . .
>
> But even assuming what I cannot assume, that some balancing is proper in this case, I feel that the Court after stating the test ignores it completely. At most it balances the right of the Government to preserve itself, against Barenblatt's right to refrain from revealing Communist affiliations. Such a balance, however mistakes the factors to be weighed. In the first place, it completely leaves out the real interest in Barenblatt's silence, the interest of people as a whole in being able to join organizations, advocate causes and make political "mistakes" without later being subjected to governmental penalties for having dared to think for themselves. It is this right to err politically,

which keeps us strong as a Nation. For no number of laws against Communism can have as much effect as the personal conviction which comes from having heard its arguments and rejected them, and from having once accepted its tenets and later recognized their worthlessness. Instead, the obloquy which results from investigations such as this not only stifles "mistakes" but prevents all but the most courageous from hazarding any views which might at some later time become disfavored. This result, whose importance cannot be overstated, is doubly crucial when it affects the universities on which we must largely rely for the experimentation and development of new ideas essential to the country's welfare. It is these interests of society, rather than Barenblatt's own right to silence, which I think the Court should put on the balance against the demands of Government, if any balancing process is to be tolerated. Instead they are not mentioned, while on the other side the demands of Government are vastly overstated and called "self preservation."

Black did not dispute Harlan's pertinency finding with which he clearly disagreed but instead concentrated on fundamental constitutional issues. He rejected the notion that legislative gloss applied to a vague law provided sufficient basis for a criminal contempt conviction. In attacking HUAC's attempts to sabotage the lives and careers of its witnesses, Black repeated Rauh's contention in *Watkins* that such actions constituted punishment by Congress, violating the separation of powers.

Douglas and Warren joined the opinion. Brennan, while expressing agreement with Black, produced his own dissent, asserting that the only purpose for the Barenblatt investigation was "exposure purely for the sake of exposure" which did not trump the First Amendment. The strongest reaction to Black's opinion came from Frankfurter, who suddenly saw a need to bolster Harlan's argument, writing to him: "I do feel strongly that at the very outset of your opinion you should

have a few pungent paragraphs putting the case in its setting."[97] Frankfurter even provided the text, incorporated by
Harlan,[98] expounding on "the far-reaching power of Congress
which we are asked to censor and curtail while at the same
time no doubt is left that we are on alert in protection of truly
academic interests." The decision was announced on June 8,
1959.[99]

(FOR THE FULL SUPREME COURT DECISION, *BARENBLATT V.
US*, SEE HTTPS://MONTHLYREVIEW.ORG/CHANDLERDAVIS).

Two months later, the panel for the Sixth Circuit, minus
Stewart, affirmed Chandler's conviction,[100] relying heavily on
the *Barenblatt* ruling. Unhappy with Wittenberg's handling
of his case, Chandler decided to pursue certiorari on his own.
His petition to the Supreme Court raised the Meiklejohn
argument that Wittenberg would not advance.[101]

Chandler subsequently had second thoughts over the
idea of representing himself.[102] With the approval of Corliss
Lamont, he made arrangements for civil rights attorney
Frank Donner to take over as counsel.[103] Donner recognized
the difficulty of obtaining certiorari for an appeal so close to
that of *Barenblatt*. He revised the petition and distinguished
Chandler's case by emphasizing the role of *Operation Mind* in
attracting the attention of HUAC.[104] It was not enough. One
of Warren's clerks offered the following analysis in his memo
on the petition:

> Since this case is identical to *Barenblatt*, the only reason I can
> see for granting cert would be the possibility of persuading
> one of the majority in *Barenblatt* to change his vote. However,
> since such a possibility is very remote, granting cert would
> only give the majority an opportunity to write more bad law in
> this area. Therefore, unless one of the five indicates a change
> of heart, I think cert ought to be denied.[105]

On December 7, 1959, with just Douglas and Black in favor,

the Supreme Court denied certiorari.[106] Five years after receiving the indictment, Chandler had exhausted his appeals. He served his six-month sentence at the federal prison in Danbury, Connecticut, where Lloyd Barenblatt was another inmate.[107]

Reviewing the court experience, a striking aspect was the integral part of (what might be called) extraneous factors in the outcome. Watkins, Davis, and Barenblatt each defied HUAC over a three-month period. Watkins and Barenblatt made it to the Supreme Court, at least partly because their trials were in the District of Columbia Circuit, which is favored for constitutional adjudication. The major differences in their cases—Watkins was responsive about himself and Barenblatt asserted the First Amendment at his hearing—were not factors in their differing verdicts.

Of considerable importance in the Appeals Court was whether Edgerton or Bastian participated in the panel. A recusal and the timing of retirements on the Supreme Court went a long way to Watkins going free and Barenblatt to prison. Finally, were it not for Frankfurter's aggressiveness in deleting a paragraph from the second draft of Warren's *Watkins* opinion, the outcome probably would have fulfilled Chandler's long-shot objective of reining in HUAC.

Few people went to prison as a consequence of *Barenblatt*. Most witnesses with CPUSA connections were taking the Fifth or naming names. Some First Amendment challengers, such as Philadelphia schoolteacher Goldie Watson, still had their convictions overturned on the basis of pertinency.[108] Carl Braden, however, tried the First Amendment in 1958, by which time HUAC was savvy to ensuring against the *Watkins* issues. He was convicted and lost his appeal three years later, in an opinion written by Stewart, on the basis of *Barenblatt*.[109]

A turning point in the prosecution of First Amendment objectors to the Communist question came in 1962, too late for Chandler who had completed his sentence. The case, *Russell v. US*,[110] involved six petitioners, reviewed together, who had been convicted separately of contempt for refusing to answer questions before HUAC and a Senate committee. Oral argument took place before the same justices who had heard *Barenblatt*. In a puzzling departure from his position on related cases, Stewart sided with the four liberals to quash the convictions, not by overturning *Barenblatt* but on the narrow point that the indictments were defective because they neglected to apprise the defendants of the question under inquiry. Warren appointed Stewart to write the opinion, presumably following the strategy of delegating ownership to lock in a tenuous vote. Then, in the interval prior to delivery of the decision on May 21, 1962, both Whittaker and Frankfurter suffered health crises. Whittaker retired and Frankfurter was incapacitated, leaving them out of the 5–2 decision. Harlan expressed disbelief, at the majority's reasoning, in his dissent with Clark.

At about the same time, folksinger Pete Seeger, who had refused to answer the Communist question in a 1955 HUAC hearing, had his conviction reversed by the Court of Appeals for the Second Circuit on the same grounds of a faulty indictment.[111] On the merits, it is difficult to reconcile the outcomes for the similarly indicted Barenblatt, Davis, Braden, Russell, and Seeger, three of whom went to prison. Most significantly, with Byron White and Arthur Goldberg replacing Whittaker and Frankfurter in 1962, the Supreme Court became more receptive to challenges based on civil liberties.

President Obama presents 2012 National Humanities Medal to
Natalie Zemon Davis at the White House.
(PHOTO BY RALPH ALSWANG, COURTESY OF THE NATIONAL ENDOWMENT
FOR THE HUMANITIES)

CHAPTER NINE

Fast Forward

The previous chapters reveal a key distinction between Chandler's prospects for a favorable outcome through the courts and via review by the University of Michigan. If circumstances or timing had been slightly different, the Supreme Court might have decided in his favor. In contrast, he never had a chance at Michigan. There, President Hatcher and both reviewing committees wholly backed his termination. Through it all, Chandler maintained his research at a standard that garnered the attention of leading mathematicians.

Even after finishing his incarceration in 1960, Chandler remained on the blacklist for tenure-track faculty positions in the United States. Nevertheless, he was creative in obtaining employment on the academy's periphery. Two years earlier, Chandler had joined the editorial staff of *Mathematical Reviews*, a periodical of the American Mathematical Society that produces abstracts of research papers and books. For this work, the Davis family, then with three children, moved to Providence, Rhode Island, where the headquarters of the Society was located.

Despite the serious handicap of losing her passport, Natalie soldiered on through the 1950s to complete her thesis research.[1]

When asked more recently whether she had ever considered giving up on doctoral degree study, Natalie responded passionately: "Never! Never, wouldn't have even thought of it! Never crossed my mind! Never, how could you even ask that?"[2] In 1959 she received her PhD in history from the University of Michigan. Natalie then began a non-tenure-track faculty position at Brown University.

Serving the sentence was a particularly stressful time for the family. Natalie, explaining to the kids that "your daddy is in prison for something good,"[3] drove them to Connecticut for regular visits with their father. The American Mathematical Society placed Chandler on leave without pay, so at least he had a job to return to. Editing abstracts of mathematical papers, however, was not the career he desired.

Mark Nickerson and other HUAC unfriendlies had found academic homes in Canada. While his case was under litigation, Chandler confined his employment search to the United States. He was determined to avoid leaving any appearance of "skipping out" on his prosecution.[4] After his release from prison, Chandler expanded his horizon. This included reaching out to the prominent University of Toronto geometer Donald Coxeter. In Chandler's words:

> Running into Coxeter at an AMS meeting, I inquired about the possibility of applying, and he responded brightly, "Oh! Would you come to Toronto?" I assured him this would interest me, he dropped a word to the Chair, and I got a good offer right away. (Things were simpler in those days.)[5]

Agreement to terms as a tenured University of Toronto associate professor was not the end of the drama for Chandler. Prior to leaving the United States, he applied for landed immigrant status to become a permanent resident of Canada. The application was rejected by the Minister of Citizenship and Immigration.[6] Chandler engaged a lawyer in Ottawa and sought the intervention of the Canadian Association of University Teachers. Uncertainty persisted sufficiently long that, no longer employed by *Mathematical Reviews*, he began the process of arranging for a temporary position in Europe. Just after sending away the movers who were engaged to transport the household goods to Canada, word arrived that a new minister had approved Chandler for landed immigrant status. In 1962 the Davis family relocated to Canada. After some time, Natalie joined the history faculty at the university.

The Toronto appointment enabled Chandler to engage fully in the activities of the mathematics profession. He succeeded handsomely in the career that he was deprived of in Ann Arbor. Chandler Davis became a major figure in the fields of linear algebra and operator theory.[7] He supervised the dissertations of fifteen doctoral students. His service to the profession included a term as vice president of the American Mathematical Society, stints on the editorial boards of research journals, and a long tenure as editor-in-chief of the periodical *The Mathematical Intelligencer*, which covered the history and culture of mathematics. Most unusual for a mathematician was the scope of Chandler's activism. He did not merely protest the Vietnam War, he also organized opposition among colleagues at meetings and traveled to North Vietnam in 1971 to support mathematics in the beleaguered country.[8]

Natalie Zemon Davis has earned acclaim as one of the foremost historians of her generation. She was called to a professorship at UC Berkeley in 1971 and moved to Princeton seven years later where she retired in 1996 as Henry Charles Lea Professor of History. Her seminal research has been recognized with awards of the Ludwig Holberg International Prize and the United States' National Humanities Medal. Zemon Davis holds honorary degrees from fifty universities and colleges, including Harvard, Princeton, Yale, Chicago, Oxford, and Cambridge. In 1987, she served as president of the American Historical Association. To the general public, Zemon Davis is best known for her book *The*

Return of Martin Guerre and her role as historical consultant behind the French film of the same name.

The successful careers of Chandler and Natalie belie the formidable obstructions they overcame. In particular, the Davises established the foundations for their research programs in the midst of the 1954 to 1962 period of Chandler's marginalization by the U.S. academy. Their scholarly resilience is astounding.

In contrast, HUAC aged much less gracefully. During the 1960s, political momentum shifted from the Red Scare to civil rights and Vietnam War protests. Unintimidated in their appearances before the committee, radicals such as Jerry Rubin and Abbie Hoffman put on outrageous displays of mockery and contempt. Among the New Left, the HUAC subpoena became a status symbol. When one less prominent activist lamented his inability to draw the attention of the committee, Rubin diagnosed the condition as "subpoenas envy."[9] The declawed HUAC became an object of ridicule. Its 1969 reboot under a new name was insufficient. Six years later Congress ended HUAC's final incarnation.

At the University of Michigan, reconsideration of the treatment accorded to Davis, Markert, and Nickerson was stimulated by discussion of their case in a 1988 campus lecture of history professor David Hollinger titled "Academic Culture at Michigan, 1938–1988: The Apotheosis of Pluralism."[10] A notable consequence was a decision by Adam Kulakow to produce a documentary film on the 1954 events for his senior honors thesis. In his research, Kulakow interviewed all of the principals.

Screenings of Kulakow's *Keeping in Mind* on campus the following spring generated interest in making some "gesture of reconciliation" to the three former faculty. After initiatives to involve Hatcher, current university president Duderstadt, and the Regents were unsuccessful, the University Senate took action on its own. Their 1990 resolution apologized for "the failure of the University Community to protect the fundamental values of intellectual freedom at that time" and created the annual University of Michigan Senate's Davis, Markert, Nickerson Lecture on Academic and Intellectual Freedom. When Markert learned that, rather than a gesture from the Regents, there would be a lecture series honoring the three sanctioned faculty, he responded: "That's better, because people will be reminded every year."[11] In 2015, President Schlissel, sixth in the office after Hatcher and third after Duderstadt, expressed regrets, discussed in the Preface of this book. The Regents have yet to repudiate their 1954 discipline.

As this was being written, I asked Chandler, who was then ninety-five, whether he was still a Marxist or if some other political classification was more apt. He responded that he was not a Marxist-Leninist but might be regarded as "some kind of Red-Green" or "ecosocialist."[12] To this day Chandler and Natalie remain resolute in the conviction that their defiance of HUAC and challenge through the justice system were correct choices.

This book tells the story of an individual's courageous stand on civil liberties before a judicial system and academy in thrall to opportunistic demagogues. As this manuscript goes to press these institutions are facing another challenge analogous to what Chandler Davis confronted. In reaction to the rising consciousness of systemic racism, some states are passing laws to muzzle teachers from conveying any viewpoint that discrimination is present in their country. For example, the Florida Individual Freedom Act prevents faculty in public universities from, among other things, expressing approval of affirmative action and advancing a view that "status [i]s either privileged or oppressed" on the basis of race or sex.

The Florida law is being touted by its champion, Governor Ron DeSantis, apparently to advance his presidential ambitions. College administrators fear, as did Harlan Hatcher, that opposing a powerful government official could be detrimental to the support of their programs. The adverse effects on higher education in Florida are already emerging.[13] In November 2022, after considering the First Amendment and academic freedom ramifications, District Judge Mark Walker blocked the law's implementation pending review by the Court of Appeals. In the eleventh circuit, where Florida lies, a majority of the sitting judges are appointees of former president Donald Trump.[14] The ultimate disposition of the repressive regulations may reach a Supreme Court greatly at variance with the ideals that Chandler Davis espoused throughout his life.

Acknowledgments

Vital resources for this book were the records made available to me at the archives listed below. In each case I have appended the names of some of the staff members whose expertise and courtesy, particularly under the challenges of Covid-19, were essential to the completion of my research.

Bentley Historical Library, University of Michigan: Diana Bachman, Sarah McLusky, Caitlin Moriarty
Library of Congress: Patrick Kerwin, Bruce Kirby
Historical and Special Collections, Harvard Law School Library: Sarah Wharton, Edwin Moloy, Lesley Schoenfeld
Special Collections, Princeton University Library: Amanda Ferrara
National Archives: Adam Berenbak

Several of my colleagues at Emory University provided valuable assistance. Jenny Vitti swiftly obtained materials through Interlibrary Loan. Political scientists Michael Giles, Harvey Klehr, and Tom Walker patiently answered a variety of questions. Law professor Michael Perry graciously permitted me to sit in on his Freedom of Speech course.

The interviews for Adam Kulakow's film research clarified a number of issues. I thank Adam for permitting me to review and quote from his materials stored in the Bentley Historical Library.

I am especially grateful to Chandler and Natalie Zemon Davis for their forbearance in undergoing interviews and a multitude of follow-up questions through email. After I completed the manuscript, Chandler read it and pointed out a few minor errors and some passages in need of clarification. He also suggested, quite appropriately, including some discussion of what now appears in the final chapter on the demise of HUAC and the creation of the Academic Freedom Lectures at the University of Michigan. Earlier partial drafts of the manuscript were reviewed by historians Ellen Schrecker and Howard Brick, who contributed insightful suggestions.

It was a pleasure to work with Michael Yates, Martin Paddio, and Rebecca Manski of Monthly Review Press.

My sister-in-law, Carol Neidle, provided technical assistance. Finally, I once again thank my wife, Ellen Neidle, for her willingness to pause her microbiological research and serve as the sounding board and IT-advisor on my fourth and final book.

Bibliography

Laurence Buermeyer et al. *An Introduction to Reflective Thinking.* Houghton Mifflin, 1923.

Steve Batterson. *Stephen Smale: The Mathematician Who Broke the Dimension Barrier.* American Mathematical Society, 2000.

Steve Batterson. *Pursuit of Genius.* A.K. Peters, 2006.

Jerome Barron and C. Thomas Dienes. *First Amendment Law in a Nutshell.* West Academic Publishing, 2018.

Carl Beck. *Contempt of Congress.* Hauser Press, 1959.

Michal Belknap. *Cold War Political Justice.* Greenwood Press, 1977.

Bob Blauner. *Resisting McCarthyism.* Stanford University Press, 2009.

Haig Bosmajian. *The Freedom Not to Speak.* New York University Press, 1999.

Larry Ceplair and Steven Englund. *The Inquisition in Hollywood.* Anchor Press, 1980.

Man-Duen Choi and Peter Rosenthal. "A Survey of Chandler Davis." *Linear Algebra and Its Applications,* 208/209 (1994): 3–18.

Chandler Davis. "So You're Going to Prison." *The Nation,* 191/19 (1960): 435–37.

Chandler Davis. "The Purge." In *A Century of Mathematics in America,* vol. 1, 413–28. American Mathematical Society, 1988.

Natalie Zemon Davis. *A Passion for History.* Truman State University Press, 2010.

Marian Rubins Davis and Horace Bancroft Davis. *Liberalism Is Not Enough.* Orca Press, 1971.

Del Dixon. *The Supreme Court in Conference (1940–1985).* Oxford University Press, 2001.

Thomas Doherty. *Show Trial.* Columbia University Press, 2018.

Theodore Draper. *The Roots of American Communism*. Viking Press, 1957.

Dwight Eisenhower. *The White House Years: Mandate for Change, 1953– 1956*. Doubleday, 1963.

Noah Feldman. *Scorpions*. Twelve, 2010.

Glenn Frankel. *High Noon*. Bloomsbury, 2017.

Michael Gerhardt. "A Tale of Two Textualists: A Critical Comparison of Justices Black and Scalia." *Boston University Law Review* 74 (1994): 25–66.

Walter Goodman. *The Committee*. Farrar, Straus and Giroux, 1968.

Mary Gray. "A Committed Life: An Interview with Chandler Davis." *Mathematical Intelligencer* 36/1 (2014): 2–5.

Erwin Griswold. *The Fifth Amendment Today*. Harvard University Press, 1955.

John Earl Haynes, Harvey Klehr, and Alexander Vassiliev. *Spies*. Yale University Press, 2009.

Adam Hochschild. *American Midnight*. Mariner Books, 2022.

Peggie Hollingsworth. *Unfettered Expression: Freedom in American Intellectual Life*. University of Michigan Press, 2000.

John Holbrook. The Mathematics of Chandler Davis. *The Mathematical Intelligencer* 36/1 (2014): 6–12.

Peter Irons. *The Courage of Their Convictions*. Free Press, 1988.

Richard Kluger. *Simple Justice*. Vintage, 2004.

Josh Lukin. "Trying to Say Something True: The Paradoxa Interview with Chandler Davis." In *It Walks in Beauty*, 290–347. Aqueduct Press, 2010.

David Maraniss. *A Good American Family*. Simon & Schuster, 2019.

David McCullough. *Truman*. Simon & Schuster, 1992.

Patrick Mears. "Of Congressional Witch-Hunts in Academia: The Case of *United States of America v Horace Chandler Davis*." *Journal of the Historical Society of the United States District Court for the Western District of Michigan* 4/2 (2006): 1–22.

Alexander Meiklejohn. *Free Speech and Its Relation to Self-Government*. Harper & Brothers, 1948.

Alexander Meiklejohn. "Freedom and the People." *The Nation*, 177/24 (1953): 500–502.

Matthew Mettler. "A Workers' Cold War in the Quad Cities: The Fate of Labor Militancy in the Farm Equipment Industry, 1949–1955." *Annals of Iowa* 68/4 (2009): 359–94.

Richard Lawrence Miller. *Whittaker: Struggles of a Supreme Court Justice*. Greenwood Press, 2002.

Calvin Moore. *Mathematics at Berkeley*. A. K. Peters, 2007.

Victor Navasky. *Naming Names*. Viking Press, 1980.

Roger Newman. *Hugo Black*. Pantheon Books, 1994.

Steve Nadis and Shing-Tung Yau. *A History in Sum*. Harvard University Press, 2013.

Michael Parrish. *Citizen Rauh*. University of Michigan Press, 2010.

William Preston. *Aliens and Dissenters*. University of Illinois Press, 1994.

Arthur Sabin. *In Calmer Times*. University of Pennsylvania Press, 1999.

Bernard Schwartz. *Super Chief*. New York University Press, 1983.

Ellen Schrecker. *No Ivory Tower*. Oxford University Press, 1986.

Ellen Schrecker. *Many Are the Crimes*. Little, Brown, 1998.

Regin Schmidt. *Red Scare*. Museum Tusculanum Press, 2000.

Steven Schiffrin, Jesse Choper, and Frederick Schauer. *The First Amendment Cases—Comments—Questions*. West Academic Publishing, 2015.

Edward Shaffer. "Repression at the University of Michigan." In *Wisconsin "Government and Business" and the History of Heterodox Economic Thought*, vol. 22-C, 195–205. Emerald Publishing, 2004.

Craig Alan Smith. *Failing Justice: Charles Evans Whittaker on the Supreme Court*. McFarland & Company, 2005.

Brad Snyder. *Democratic Justice*. W. W. Norton, 2022.

Robert Stripling. *The Red Plot Against America*. Arno Press, 1977.

Athan Theoharis and John Cox. *The Boss*. Temple University Press, 1988.

Athan Theoharis. *Spying on Americans*. Temple University Press, 1978.

Athan Theoharis. *Chasing Spies*. Ivan R. Dee, 2002.

Melvin Urofsky. *Felix Frankfurter: Judicial Restraint and Individual Liberties*. Twayne Publishers, 1991.

G. Edward White. *Earl Warren: A Public Life*. Oxford University Press, 1982.

Tom Wicker. *One of Us*. Random House, 1991.

David Williams. "The Bureau of Investigation and Its Critics, 1919–1921: The Origins of Federal Political Surveillance." *Journal of American History* 68/3 (1981): 560–79.

Tinsley Yarbrough. *John Marshall Harlan*. Oxford University Press, 1992.

Ed Yellin and Jean Fagan Yellin. *In Contempt*. Alte Books, 2020.

Notes

Foreword

1. See https://monthlyreview.org/ChandlerDavis for the text of that decision, *Barenblatt v. United States*, 360 U.S. 109, 1959.

Preface

1. Ellen Schrecker, *No Ivory Tower* (Oxford: Oxford University Press, 1986), chap. 8, " 'The Slow Treatment': Academic Committees and Their Unfriendly Witnesses."
2. *Barenblatt v. United States,* 360 U.S. 109 (1959).
3. Schrecker, *No Ivory Tower*.
4. President Schlissel's "Remarks at 2015 Winter Commencement" on his University of Michigan website, December 20, 2015.

1. Red Diaper Baby

1. "Instructor" is a faculty rank that is less common today. It is below assistant professor.
2. This paragraph and the next are based largely on Ellen Schrecker, *No Ivory Tower* (Oxford: Oxford University Press, 1986); and the House Un-American Activities Committee files on Chandler Davis, Clement Markert, Lawrence Klein, Mark Nickerson, and Nate Coburn at the National Archives, Washington, D.C.
3. Throughout this narrative the abbreviation CPUSA will be used to represent the Communist Party that Americans joined. At various times this organization went by names characterized by other abbreviations, such as CP.

4. The remainder of this chapter is largely based on Marion Rubins Davis and Horace Bancroft Davis, *Liberalism Is Not Enough* (Victoria, BE: Orca Press, 1971) and the author's interview with Chandler Davis on March 29, 2014.

5. Davis and Davis, *Liberalism Is Not Enough*, 146.

6. H. B. Davis, "Academic Freedom in Pittsburgh," *New Republic*, Vol. 59 (May 22, 1929), 21-22.

7. Laurence Buermeyer, et. al., *An Introduction to Reflective Thinking* (Boston: Houghton Mifflin Company, 1923).

8. Davis and Davis, *Liberalism Is Not Enough*, 41.

9. Email to author from Chandler Davis, February 2, 2017.

10. Escola Livre Sociologia e Politica de São Paulo.

11. Chandler Davis interview with author, March 29, 2014.

12. Psychologist Harrison Harley would later direct the Communist-associated Samuel Adams School and be called to testify before the Senate Internal Security Sobcommittee.

2. Risky Behavior

1. This chapter relies heavily on interviews with Chandler Davis on March 29, 2014, and July 27 and July 28, 2017, as well as emails between the author and Davis over 2016-2018.

2. Davis and Davis, *Liberalism Is Not Enough*.

3. Ibid.

4. Josh Lukin, "Trying to Say Something True: The Paradoxa Interview with Chandler Davis," in Josh Lukin, editor, *It Walks in Beauty: Selected Prose of Chandler Davis* (Seattle, WA: Aqueduct Press, 2010), 290-347.

5. Email from Chandler Davis to author, October 11, 2017.

6. The FBI files I obtained on Chandler Davis were from the Headquarters and Boston offices. The FBI stated that some records which may have been responsive to the request had been destroyed. No files were available from the Detroit bureau.

7. Memorandum by Frederick Connors in Chandler Davis FBI files, March 28, 1947.

8. Memorandum by Special Agent Richard Dow in Chandler Davis FBI files, May 8, 1947.

9. Information on Natalie Zemon Davis is drawn largely from an interview of her by the author on July 28, 2017, and her American Council of Learned Society's Charles Homer Haskins Lecture for 1997 in Philadelphia titled "A Life of Learning."

10. Interview with Natalie Zemon Davis, July 28, 2017.

11. Nancy Zemon Davis, Charles Homer Haskins Lecture.

12. Interview with Natalie Zemon Davis, July 28, 2017.

13. Natalie Zemon Davis, Charles Homer Haskins Lecture for 1997.

14. The remainder of this chapter relies on Chandler Davis, "The Purge," in *A Century of Mathematics in America*, vol. 1 (Providence, RI: American

Mathematical Society, 1988), 413-28; Ellen Schrecker, *No Ivory Tower*; Chandler's FBI files as well as the interviews and email with Chandler Davis.

15. Memorandum by Special Agent Connors in Chandler Davis FBI files, March 7, 1949.

16. Ibid.

17. Report on Chandler Davis by Thomas McLaughlin in Chandler Davis FBI files, June 2, 1949.

18. Davis, "The Purge," 419.

19. Email from Chandler Davis to author, January 4, 2018.

20. On the University of California loyalty oath see, for example, Bob Blauner, *Resisting McCarthyism* (Redwood City, CA: Stanford University Press, 2009}; Schrecker, *No Ivory Tower*; and Calvin Moore, *Mathematics at Berkeley* (Natick, MA: A. K. Peters, Ltd, 2007).

21. Davis, "The Purge," 420.

3. The CPUSA and the United States Government

1. Information on Hoover is drawn from Athan Theoharis and John Cox, *The Boss* (Philadelphia: Temple University Press, 1988); Regin Schmidt, *Red Scare* (Copenhagen: Museum Tusculum Press, 2000); William Preston, *Aliens and Dissenters* (Urbana: University of Illinois Press, 1994); Ellen Schrecker, *Many Are the Crimes* (Boston: Little, Brown, 1998).

2. Theoharis and Cox, *The Boss*, 48-49.

3. Adam Hochschild, *American Midnight* (New York: Mariner Press, 2022).

4. Schmidt, *Red Scare*, 161.

5. Ibid., 276-78.

6. The early history of the CPUSA is drawn from Theodore Draper, *The Roots of American Communism* (New York: Viking Press, 1957).

7. Schmidt, *Red Scare*, 280.

8. Theoharis and Cox, *The Boss*, 58.

9. See Theoharis and Cox, *The Boss*.

10. Further details on the abuses are available in Theoharis and Cox, *The Boss*; and Schmidt, *Red Scare*.

11. For more on Post and his role see Hochschild, *American Midnight*.

12. For details on these investigations, discovered decades later, see David Williams, "The Bureau of Investigation and Its Critics, 1919-1921: The Origins of Political Surveillance," *Journal of American History* 68/33 (1981): 560-79.

13. Hochschild, *American Midnight*, 313-22.

14. Theoharis and Cox, *The Boss*, 64.

15. Schmidt, *Red Scare*, 293; and Draper, *The Roots of American Communism*, 205-8.

16. Draper, *The Roots of American Communism*, 388-90.

17. Theoharis and Cox, *The Boss*, 71-72.

18. Schmidt, *Red Scare*, 322; and Theoharis and Cox, *The Boss*, 76.

19. Schmidt, *Red Scare*, 324–25; and Theoharis and Cox, *The Boss*, 83–85.

20. Theoharis and Cox, *Red Scare*, 83–84.

21. For different views on the extent of Hoover's deception see Schmidt, *Red Scare*, 325–28; and Theoharis and Cox, *The Boss*, 92–93.

22. Schmidt, *Red Scare*, 329.

23. Ibid., 136–46.

24. Ibid., 329-30.

25. Theoharis and Cox, *The Boss*, 148–53.

26. The principal reference for HUAC is Walter Goodman, *The Committee* (New York: Farrar, Straus and Giroux, 1968).

27. According to John Earl Haynes, Harvey Klehr, and Alexander Vassiliev, *Spies* (New Haven: Yale University Press, 2009), 285–87, Dickstein was on the payroll of a Soviet spy organization, receiving monthly stipends in the late 1930s.

28. Michal Belknap, *Cold War Political Justice* (Westport, CT: Greenwood Press, 1977), 16; and Goodman, *The Committee*, 14.

29. On the Smith Act see Belknap, *Cold War Political Justice*.

30. Tom Wicker, *One of Us* (New York: Random House, 1991), 34–48.

31. Schmidt, *Red Scare*.

32. Goodman, *The Committee*, 65.

33. Schmidt, *Red Scare*, 341–34 and 349–55.

34. Athan Theoharis, *Chasing Spies* (Chicago: Ivan R. Dee, 2002), 57, lists break-ins, wiretaps, bugs, and mail openings.

35. Ibid., 59 and 151–63.

36. References for the 1947 Hollywood hearings are Thomas Doherty, *Show Trial* (New York: Columbia University Press, 2018); Larry Ceplair and Steven Englund, *The Inquisition in Hollywood* (Garden City, NY: Anchor Press, 1980); Walter Goodman, *The Committee*; Glenn Frankel, *High Noon* (New York: Bloomsbury, 2017); Victor Navasky, *Naming Names* (New York: Viking Press, 1980); Carl Beck, *Contempt of Congress* (New Orleans: Hauser Press, 1959). The list of the 43 subpoenaed is in John Doherty, *Show Trial*, 85. Transcripts of testimony for these and other HUAC hearings are available via LexisNexis.

37. Ronald Reagan demurred on whether being a Communist should become illegal.

38. The three movies were *Mission to Moscow, Song of Russia,* and *The North Star*.

39. The Hollywood Ten were John Howard Lawson, Albert Maltz, Dalton Trumbo, Alvah Bessie, Samuel Ornitz, Herbert Biberman, Edward Dmytryk, Adrian Scott, Ring Lardner Jr., and Lester Cole.

40. Among the considerable literature see Steven Schifrin et al., *The First Amendment Cases* (St. Paul: West Academic Publishing, 2001); and Jerome Barron and C. Thomas Dienes, *First Amendment Law in a Nutshell* (St. Paul: West Academic Publishing, 2018).

41. Doherty, *Show Trial*, 206.
42. For more on Lawson see Ceplair and Englund, *The Inquisition in Hollywood*.
43. Interspersed with the testimonies by the Hollywood Ten were a few witnesses, such as producer Dore Schary, who were trying to be supportive of both sides in the proceedings.
44. Robert Stripling, *The Red Plot Against America* (New York: Arno Press, 1977), 75.
45. Theoharis, *Chasing Spies*, 166–67.
46. *Lawson v. United States,* 176 F.2d 49 (DC Cir. 1949).
47. Thomas Doherty, *Show Trial*, 324.
48. More on the possible motivations behind the actions can be found in Thomas Doherty, *Show Trial*, and the references in note 36.
49. For further details see David McCullough, *Truman* (New York: Simon and Schuster, 1992), chap. 12: "Turning Point."
50. The remainder of the chapter draws heavily from Belknap, *Cold War Political Justice*.
51. Ibid., 47.
52. Ibid., 80–82.
53. *Dennis v. United States,* 183 F.2d 201 (2d Cir 1950).
54. *Schenk v. United States,* 249 US 47 (1919).
55. *Whitney v. California,* 274 US 357 (1927).
56. *Dennis v. United States,* 341 US 494 (1951).
57. Belknap, *Cold War Political Justice*, 157.
58. *Yates v. United States,* 354 US 298 (1957).
59. Schmidt, *Red Scare*, 190.

4. Scrutiny in Ann Arbor

1.   On Brauer and Bott and their standing among Harvard mathematicians see Steve Nadis and Shing-Tung Yau, *A History in Sum* (Cambridge, MA: Harvard University Press, 1913).
2.   On Smale see Steve Batterson, *Stephen Smale: The Mathematician Who Broke the Dimension Barrier* (Providence, RI: American Mathematical Society, 2000).
3.   For a discussion of front groups, some of which had more CPUSA involvement than the Ann Arbor Council of Arts, Sciences, and Professions, see Schrecker, *Many Are the Crimes*.
4.   Natalie Zemon Davis, *A Passion for History* (Kirksville, MO: Truman State University Press, 2010), 140.
5.   An additional sponsor of the pamphlet was a student group, the Civil Liberties Committee of the University of Michigan.
6.   Memorandum to FBI Director in Chandler Davis FBI files, May 31, 1955.
7.   Theoharis, in *Chasing Spies*, 160–63, gives a description of blind memoranda that the FBI prepared on suspects for HUAC investigations. A description of *Operation Mind* is included in what fits the profile of a blind memorandum

that is among the Horace Chandler Davis materials in the Records of the House Un-American Activities, National Archives, Washington D. C.

8. Details of the incident, beyond the description given, are available in Batterson, *Stephen Smale: The Mathematician Who Broke the Dimension Barrier* and in 1952 issues of the *Michigan Daily.*

9. *Michigan* Daily, December 18, 1952.

10. *Michigan* Daily, December 18, 1952.

11. *Michigan Daily*, March 7, 1952.

12. Email from Chandler Davis to author, June 19, 2019.

13. *Michigan Daily*, June 25, 1952.

14. No reference to Chandler's collaboration with Keniston appears in his FBI and HUAC records.

15. That Rozian was the informant is confirmed in a memorandum from SAC, Detroit, to Director, FBI, in Chandler Davis FBI files, March 16, 1959.

16. Memorandum from SAC, Detroit, to Director, FBI, in Chandler Davis FBI files, May 27, 1952. It seems likely that the parenthetical remark was provided by the FBI rather than Rozian.

17. Memoranda from John Edgar Hoover in Chandler Davis FBI files, June 23, 1952, and June 28, 1952.

18. Email from Chandler Davis to author, April 1, 2019.

19. See post of Natalie Davis, "How the FBI turned me on to rare books," *New York Review of Books* blog, NYR Daily (July 30, 2013).

20. See previously referenced 1952 FBI memoranda involving Director Hoover; and FBI report on Chandler Davis by Kenneth Haser in Chandler Davis FBI files, 5, July 17, 1953.

21. There were actually two Ann Arbor individuals providing the FBI with information on Chandler. In a report by Robert Rangeley in the Chandler Davis FBI files, March 16, 1954, the informants are listed as T2 and T4. T2, who disclosed the 1952 travel plans, is Rozian. T4, whose disclosures indicated less personal connection, is unknown to the Davises, and may well have been a student.

22. Email from Chandler Davis to author, July 21, 2019.

23. Schrecker, *No Ivory Tower*, 61.

24. Email from Chandler Davis to author, March 28, 2019.

25. Chandler Davis, "The Purge," 420.

26. Memo from Donald Appell to Louis Russell on Horace Chandler Davis, December 9, 1953, Records of the House Un-American Activities Committee, National Archives, Washington, DC.

27. Clement Lawrence Markert, Records of the House Un-American Activities Committee, National Archives, Washington, DC.

28. Memo from Donald Appell to Louis Russell on Nathaniel Coburn, December 9, 1953, Records of the House Un-American Activities Committee, National Archives, Washington, DC.

29. Memo from Donald Appell to Louis Russell on Mark Nickerson, December

10, 1953, Records of the House Un-American Activities Committee, National Archives, Washington, DC.

30. Lawrence Robert Klein, Records of the House Un-American Activities Committee, National Archives, Washington, DC.

31. On Klein's time at Michigan and the discussions about his promotion see Chairman's proposal for appointment, January 13, 1955, Box 4, Marvin Niehuss Papers; and Charles Odegaard to Vice President Niehuss, March 31, 1955, Box 5, Marvin Niehuss Papers, both in Bentley Historical Library, University of Michigan.

32. Telegram from Hatcher to HUAC chair Harold Velde reprinted in "President's Report to the University Senate on the Procedures and Actions Involving Three Members of the University Faculty," October 5, 1954, Box 6, Marvin Niehuss Papers, Bentley Historical Library, University of Michigan.

33. Interview with Chandler Davis, March 29, 2014. Some time after receiving his subpoena Davis met with Hatcher to inform him of the situation. Hatcher revealed to Davis that the original list of suspects was much larger.

34. On the Niehuss mission to Washington see the interviews with Harlan Hatcher and Marvin Niehuss in the Adam Kulakow Papers, Bentley Historical Library, University of Michigan.

5. Deciding on a Response to HUAC

1. 340 US 159 (1950).
2. Beck, *Contempt of Congress*, 85.
3. 340 US 367 (1951).
4. On the waiver doctrine see Erwin Griswold, *The Fifth Amendment Today* (Cambridge, MA: Harvard University Press, 1955), 22-24.
5. Frankel, *High Noon*.
6. Ibid., 131.
7. Ibid., 133-34.
8. David Maraniss, in *A Good American Family* (New York: Simon & Schuster, 2019) narrates the nomadic plight of his family after his journalist father took the Fifth in the 1952 Detroit hearing, was fired by the *Detroit Times*, and moved around the country among the few periodicals willing to employ him.
9. For examples and further discussion, see Schrecker, *No Ivory Tower*, 212-17.
10. Goodman, *The Committee*, 321.
11. Schrecker, *No Ivory Tower*, 218.
12. The full statement is in the *New York Times*, March 31, 1953. Its background is discussed in Schrecker, *No Ivory Tower*, 187-89.
13. *Harvard Crimson*, June 10, 1953.
14. For discussion of a number of individual cases see Schrecker, *No Ivory Tower*.
15. Ibid., 221.

16. The remainder of this chapter draws from March 29, 2014, July 27, 2017, and July 28, 2017, interviews by the author with Chandler Davis as well as emails between the author and Davis over 2016 to 2019; and interviews of Chandler Davis by Adam Kulakow in the Adam Kulakow Papers, Bentley Historical Library, University of Michigan.

17. See memo from the Department of Zoology to the Dean and the Executive Committee, April 30, 1956, and letter from Charles Odegaard to Vice President Niehuss, May 8, 1956, both in Box 5, Marvin Niehuss Papers, Bentley Historical Library, University of Michigan. Apparently Hatcher and Niehuss did not share their advance notice of the subpoenas with Charles Odegaard, Dean of the College of Literature, Science, and the Arts.

18. Email from Chandler Davis to author, November 12, 2019.

19. Testimony of Horace Davis in *Subversive Influence in the Educational Process, Part 12, Hearings Before the Subcommittee to Investigate the Administration of the Internal Security Act and Other Internal Security Laws* (Washington, DC: US Government Printing Office, 1953), 1114–21.

20. For different perspectives on Horace's firing and his unsuccessful court challenge see Davis and Davis, *Liberalism Is Not Enough*; Richard Lawrence Miller, *Whittaker: Struggles of a Supreme Court Justice* (Westport, CT: Greenwood Press, 2002); Craig Alan Smith, *Failing Justice: Charles Evans Whittaker on the Supreme Court* (Jefferson, NC: McFarland & Company, 2005).

21. See unpublished article by Chandler Davis, "Family in Blacklist Days," September 21, 2015; and, for example, the caption under Horace Davis's photo in *Kansas City Star*, 7, September 23, 1953.

22. Davis, "Family in Blacklist Days."

23. Haig Bosmajian, *The Freedom Not to Speak* (New York: New York University Press, 1999).

24. F.2d 49 (DC Cir. 1949).

25. *Barsky v. United States*, 167 F.2d 241 (DC Cir. 1948).

26. 165 F.2d 82 (2d Cir. 1948).

27. Ceplair and Englund, *The Inquisition in Hollywood*, 348–49.

28. Arthur Sabin, *In Calmer Times* (Philadelphia: University of Pennsylvania Press, 1999).

29. On Ann Fagan Ginger see her interview with Patrick Mears in *Stereoscope, the Journal of the Historical Society of the United States District Court for the Western District of Michigan* (Winter 2012), 12–16.

30. The following discussion of Meiklejohn's theory is drawn from Alexander Meiklejohn, *Free Speech and Its Relation to Self-Government* (New York: Harper & Brothers, 1953); and Alexander Meiklejohn, "Freedom and the People," *The Nation* 177/24 (1953): 500–502.

31. Ming was a member of the NAACP team that worked successfully to overturn *Plessy v. Ferguson*. See Richard Kluger, *Simple Justice* (New York: Vintage Books, 2004), 640–45. He also defended Martin Luther King Jr. in

1960 against perjury charges. Ming was the first African American full-time faculty member of the University of Chicago Law School.

32.   Chandler Davis, interview with author, March 29, 2014.
33.   Mary Gray, "A Committed Life: An Interview with Chandler Davis by Mary Gray," *Mathematical Intelligencer*, 36/1 (2014): 3.

6. The 1954 HUAC Hearings

1.   *Detroit Free Press*, 15, September 14, 1952.
2.   Klein's testimony is available in *Investigation of Communist Activities in the State of Michigan, Part 1 (Detroit)* (Washington, DC: United States Government Printing Office, 1954).
3.   All testimony is available in *Investigation of Communist Activities in the State of Michigan, Part 6 (Lansing)* (Washington, DC: United States Government Printing Office, 1954). Moulder left in the middle of the session.
4.   Schrecker, *No Ivory Tower*, 223.
5.   Ibid., 34.
6.   For more on Markert see his National Academy of Sciences Biographical Memoir: Gerald Kidder, "Clement Lawrence Markert 1917–1999," *Biographical Memoirs* 83 (2003): 3–21.
7.   In Markert's FBI files is a transcript of a January 6, 1945, interview with the Merchant Marine where Markert was asked why he was rejected for service. He states that the reason given to him was a too-rapid heartbeat, but he was certain that it was due to his participation in the Spanish Civil War.
8.   The files obtained are from the headquarters, Detroit and Denver offices. Records from the Baltimore and Los Angeles offices have not yet been accessioned to the National Archives and Records Administration.
9.   Report by J. Allmon Jr. in Clement Markert FBI files, July 2, 1942.
10.   Report by Marcus Bright in Clement Markert FBI files, September 4, 1942.
11.   Report by Marcus Bright in Clement Markert FBI files, February 27, 1943.
12.   Theoharis and Cox, *The Boss*, 172–74.
13.   Report by Marcus Bright in Clement Markert FBI files, February 27, 1943.
14.   Report by James Mason in Clement Markert FBI files, May 5, 1943.
15.   A trash cover was an FBI technique that involved examining a suspect's garbage. Report by Paul Sterner in Clement Markert FBI files, September 12, 1952.
16.   Memorandum on custodial detention in Clement Markert FBI files, June 6, 1943.
17.   Theoharis and Cox, *The Boss*, 173.
18.   Markert interview transcript, January 6, 1945; and letter from Naval Intelligence officer J. Coddington to FBI agent E. Conroy, January 18, 1945, both in Clement Markert FBI files.
19.   Report by William Pfeiffer in Clement Markert FBI files, December 3, 1948. Because FBI records from the Baltimore and Los Angeles offices are unavailable, the Bureau's perception of Markert's activity in the late 1940s is less clear than in other periods.

20. Report by Paul Sterner in Clement Markert FBI files, September 12, 1952.
21. Athan Theoharis, *Spying on Americans* (Philadelphia: Temple University Press, 1978), 48.
22. Memorandum from SAC, Los Angeles, to Director, FBI, in Clement Markert FBI files, October 20, 1950.
23. The Hollywood Arts, Sciences, and Professions Council was unaffiliated with the Council of Arts, Sciences and Professions in Ann Arbor to which Chandler and Natalie belonged.
24. Report by Marcus Bright in Clement Markert FBI files, February 24, 1950.
25. Memorandum from SAC, Detroit, to Director, FBI, in Clement Markert FBI files, August 10, 1951.
26. Letter from Director to SAC, Detroit, in Clement Markert FBI files, August 24, 1951.
27. Clement Markert file, Records of the House Un-American Activities Committee, National Archives, Washington, DC.
28. Chandler Davis file, Records of the House Un-American Activities Committee, National Archives, Washington, DC.
29. Daughter Hannah was born on November 24, 1954.
30. Interview of Chandler Davis by author, March 29, 2014.
31. Interview of Chandler Davis by author, March 29, 2014.
32. On Eisler see Schrecker, *Many Are the Crimes*.
33. Email from Natalie Zemon Davis, March 14, 2020.
34. Report by Robert Rangeley in Chandler Davis FBI files, March 14, 1954.
35. Biographical information on Watkins is included in his HUAC testimony which is available in *Investigation of Communist Activities in the Chicago Area, Part 3* (Washington, DC: United States Government Printing Office, 1954).
36. On Watkins's labor activity in the FE see Matthew Mettler, "A Workers Cold War in the Quad Cities: The Fate of Labor Militancy in the Farm Equipment Industry," *Annals of Iowa* 68 (Fall 2009): 359–94.
37. Michael Parrish, *Citizen Rauh* (Ann Arbor: University of Michigan Press, 2010).
38. Testimony by Barenblatt and others from this session is available in *Communist Methods of Infiltration (Education—Part 9)* (Washington, DC: United States Government Printing Office, 1954).
39. Biographical information on Barenblatt is drawn from Peter Irons, *The Courage of Their Convictions* (New York: Free Press, 1988).
40. Irons, *The Courage of Their Convictions*, 99–100.

7. University of Michigan Reviews

1. "President's Report to the University Senate on the Procedures and Actions Involving Three Members of the University Faculty by Harlan Hatcher," October 5, 1954, Box 6, Marvin Niehuss Papers, Bentley Historical Library, University of Michigan.

2. Press release, May 10, 1954, University of Michigan News Service, Box 2, Marvin Niehuss Papers, Bentley Historical Library, University of Michigan.

3. The AAUP Report is published in "The University of Michigan," *AAUP Bulletin* 44 (Spring 1958), 53-101.

4. AAUP Report, 56-57.

5. Email from Chandler Davis to author, May 15, 2020.

6. Interview of Natalie Zemon Davis by author, July 28, 2017, and email from Zemon Davis, May 19, 2019.

7. For further details see the AAUP Report.

8. For the full statement of Section 5.101 see the AAUP Report.

9. For Nickerson there was the Executive Committee of the Medical School.

10. The June 1, 1954, statement of the Executive Committee is in Appendix G2 of the *Faculty Working Group on Regents' Bylaws 5.09 and 5.10 Part I & II Final Recommendations*, submitted to Provost Alcock et al., February 16, 2020.

11. The Executive Committee of the Medical School first interviewed Nickerson on May 24, twelve days later.

12. No transcript was recorded, but on June 8, 1954 the Executive Committee described their discussion in a meeting with the Special Advisory Committee to the President. This transcript is available in Box 21, Marvin Niehuss Papers, Bentley Historical Library, University of Michigan.

13. Transcript of Proceedings of meeting of Special Advisory Committee to the President with Executive Committee, June 8, 1954, Box 21, Marvin Niehuss Papers, Bentley Historical Library, University of Michigan.

14. Ibid., 54.

15. Ibid., 7-12.

16. June 1, 1954 statement of the Executive Committee, Appendix G2.

17. "President's Report to the University Senate on the Procedures and Actions Involving Three Members of the University Faculty," October 5, 1954, Box 6, Marvin Niehuss Papers, Bentley Historical Library, University of Michigan.

18. Ibid.

19. AAUP Report, 62.

20. Proceedings at a Meeting of the Special Advisory Committee to the President, June 7, 1954, Box 21, Marvin Niehuss Papers, Bentley Historical Library, University of Michigan.

21. Ibid., 9-10.

22. AAUP Report, 62.

23. Notes from meeting in president's office of Appell with Ad Hoc Committee, June 2, 1954, Box 21, Marvin Niehuss Papers, Bentley Historical Library, University of Michigan.

24. "Report of Special Advisory Committee to the President," July 13, 1954, Box 6, Marvin Niehuss Papers, Bentley Historical Library, University of Michigan.

25. Smale's story is told in Batterson, *Stephen Smale*, 32.

26. Transcript of proceedings of meeting of Special Advisory Committee to the President with Executive Committee of the College of Literature, Science, and the Arts, June 8, 1954, Box 21, Marvin Niehuss Papers, Bentley Historical Library, University of Michigan.

27. Ibid., 54–55.

28. Transcript of proceedings of meeting of Special Advisory Committee to the President with Executive Committee of the Medical School, June 7, 1954, Box 21, Marvin Niehuss Papers, Bentley Historical Library, University of Michigan.

29. Ibid., 60–64. No record has been found of the particulars of Seevers's allegation.

30. Mark Nickerson interview in Adam Kulakow Papers, Bentley Historical Library, University of Michigan.

31. David Bohr interview in Adam Kulakow Papers, Bentley Historical Library, University of Michigan.

32. Transcript of proceedings of meeting of Special Advisory Committee to the President with the Executive Committee of the Mathematics Department, June 8, 1954, Box 21, Marvin Niehuss Papers, Bentley Historical Library, University of Michigan.

33. Email from Chandler Davis to author, June 9, 2020.

34. Transcript of proceedings of meeting of Special Advisory Committee to the President with the Executive Committee of the Mathematics Department, June 8, 1954, Box 21, Marvin Niehuss Papers, Bentley Historical Library, University of Michigan.

35. Ibid., 49.

36. Statement of Chandler Davis to the Special Advisory Committees to the President, June 14, 1954, Box 21, Marvin Niehuss Papers, Bentley Historical Library, University of Michigan.

37. Proceedings at a meeting of the Special Advisory Committee to the President on the suspension of Chandler Davis, June, 15, 1954, Box 21, Marvin Niehuss Papers, Bentley Historical Library, University of Michigan.

38. Ibid., 29–30.

39. Ibid., 55–56.

40. Ibid., 69–71.

41. Ibid. 72–74.

42. What Smith might have responded, and did not, was that the belief was that *many* Communists shared the trait, rather than *all*.

43. Proceedings at meeting of the Special Advisory Committee to the President on the Suspension of Chandler Davis, June 15, 1954, Box 21, Marvin Niehuss Papers, Bentley Historical Library, University of Michigan, 94–100.

44. "Report of the Special Committee to the President," July 13, 1954, Box 6, Marvin Niehuss Papers, Bentley Historical Library, University of Michigan.

45. Ibid., 19–29.

46. Proceedings at meeting of the Special Advisory Committee to the President

on the Suspension of Chandler Davis, June 15, 1954, Box 21, Marvin Niehuss Papers, Bentley Historical Library, University of Michigan, 51–53.

47. Schrecker, *No Ivory Tower*, 227–28.

48. Hatcher to Davis (with last paragraph on appeal options omitted), July 27, 1954, Box 21, Marvin Niehuss Papers, Bentley Historical Library, University of Michigan.

49. "President's Report to the University Senate on the Procedures and Actions Involving Three Members of the University Faculty," October 5, 1954, Box 6, Marvin Niehuss Papers, Bentley Historical Library, University of Michigan.

50. AAUP Report, 82.

51. Ibid., 67.

52. "President's Report to the University Senate on the Procedures and Actions Involving Three Members of the University Faculty," October 5, 1954, Box 6, Marvin Niehuss Papers, Bentley Historical Library, University of Michigan.

53. AAUP Report, 71.

54. Letter from SAC, Detroit, to Director, FBI, in Clement Markert FBI files, August 6, 1954.

55. AAUP Report, 93.

56. Dear Colleague letter from Chandler Davis, July 31, 1954, Box 27, Marvin Niehuss Papers, Bentley Historical Library, University of Michigan.

57. Proceedings of the Chandler Davis appeal hearing before the Committee on Intellectual Freedom and Integrity, Box 21, August 11, 1954, Marvin Niehuss Papers, Bentley Historical Library, University of Michigan.

58. Ibid., 8.

59. Ibid., 15.

60. Ibid., 12.

61. AAUP Report, 94.

62. Peggie Hollingsworth, *Unfettered Expression: Freedom in American Intellectual Life* (Ann Arbor: University of Michigan Press, 2000), 6.

63. Confidential letter from H. H. Saunderson to Harlan Hatcher, September 1, 1954, Box 21, Marvin Niehuss Papers, Bentley Historical Library, University of Michigan.

64. Confidential letter from Harlan Hatcher to H. H. Saunderson, September 7, 1954, Box 21, Marvin Niehuss Papers, Bentley Historical Library, University of Michigan.

65. Clement Markert interview in Adam Kulakow Papers, Bentley Historical Library, University of Michigan.

66. Marvin Niehuss to Herbert Watkins, June 24, 1955, Box 6, Marvin Niehuss Papers, Bentley Historical Library, University of Michigan.

67. Recommendation by Dugald Brown to the Dean and Executive Committee for the promotion of Clement Markert, April 30, 1956, Box 5, Marvin Niehuss Papers, Bentley Historical Library, University of Michigan.

68. Schrecker, *No Ivory Tower*, 248.

69. Dugald Brown to Dean Niehuss, June 4, 1956, Box 5, Marvin Niehuss Papers, University of Michigan.

70. Abel Wolman to Harlan Hatcher, September 12, 1956, Box 6, Marvin Niehuss Papers, Bentley Historical Library, University of Michigan.

71. Marvin Niehuss to Abel Wolman, September 26, 1956, Box 6, Marvin Niehuss Papers, Bentley Historical Library, University of Michigan.

72. For further information on Klein's scholarship see Erich Pinzon Fuchs, "Economics as a 'tooled' discipline: Lawrence R. Klein and the making of macroeconometric modeling, 1939–1959," PhD diss., Economics and Finance, Université Panthéon-Sorbonne Paris I, 2017.

73. See Chairman's proposal for appointment, January 13, 1955, Box 4, Marvin Niehuss Papers, Bentley Historical Library, University of Michigan. This discussion of the Klein promotion case is largely based on records from two collections at the Bentley Historical Library which include the Lawrence Klein folders in Boxes 4 and 5 of the Marvin Niehuss Papers and the 1979 history and interviews by Marjorie Brazer in Box 5 of the Department of Economics (University of Michigan) records ,1915–1980. Brazer had access to certain materials that are not presently available.

74. Ackley to the Dean and Executive Committee, March 18, 1955, Box 4, Marvin Niehuss Papers, Bentley Historical Library, University of Michigan.

75. Odegaard to Niehuss, March 31, 1955, Box 5, Marvin Niehuss Papers, Bentley Historical Library, University of Michigan.

76. Niehuss to Odegaard, June 8, 1955, Box 4, Marvin Niehuss Papers, Bentley Historical Library, University of Michigan.

77. Memo from Ackley to Niehuss, June 9, 1955, Box 4, Marvin Niehuss Papers, Bentley Historical Library, University of Michigan.

78. Paton to Bix (Niehuss), August 2, 1955, Box 5, Marvin Niehuss Papers, Bentley Historical Library, University of Michigan.

79. Notes on conversation with Coghlan of the FBI, September 1, 1955, Box 5, Marvin Niehuss Papers, Bentley Historical Library, University of Michigan.

80. Ackley to Odegaard, October 25, 1955, Box 5, Marvin Niehuss Papers, Bentley Historical Library, University of Michigan.

81. Niehuss to Klein, November 14, 1955, Box 5, Marvin Niehuss Papers, Bentley Historical Library, University of Michigan.

82. Klein to Niehuss, December 9, 1955, Box 5, Marvin Niehuss Papers, Bentley Historical Library, University of Michigan.

83. See David Hollinger, "Postscript 2009: Corrections and Second Thoughts," https://www.rackham.umich.edu/downloads/HollingerPostscript.pdf.

84. Drafts of Brazer's history and transcripts of her interviews are in Box 5, Department of Economics records 1915–1980, Bentley Historical Library, University of Michigan.

85. Ackley to Dean Sawyer, December 13, 1954, Box 4, Marvin Niehuss Papers. Bentley Historical Library, University of Michigan.

86. Clardy to Hatcher, May 21, 1954, Box 21, Marvin Niehuss Papers, Bentley Historical Library, University of Michigan.
87. Ackley to Dean Sawyer, December 13, 1954, Box 4, Marvin Niehuss Papers. Bentley Historical Library, University of Michigan.
88. For further discussion and examples, see Schrecker, *No Ivory Tower*.
89. Sharpe to Kenneth Boulding, August 27, 1991, copy provided by Sharpe to the author.
90. Sharpe founded the publishing company M. E. Sharpe Inc., which was sold to Routledge in 2014.
91. The remainder of this paragraph and the next are drawn from Edward Shaffer, "Repression at the University of Michigan," *Wisconsin "Government and Business" and the History of Heterodox Economic Thought* 22-C (Bingley, UK: Emerald Publishing Group, 2004), 195–205.
92. Further details are available in Batterson, *Stephen Smale*, 36–37.
93. Ibid.

8. The Path to the Supreme Court

1. On Earl Warren and the Supreme Court see Bernard Schwartz, *Super Chief* (New York: New York University Press, 1983); and G. Edward White, *Earl Warren: A Public Life* (New York: Oxford University Press, 1982).
2. Following a tip from an informant, the FBI obtained a list of donors from the Ann Arbor bank where the funds were being held. Letter to Director, FBI, concerning Emergency Fund Committee for Horace Chandler Davis in Chandler Davis FBI files, September 21, 1955.
3. Email from Chandler Davis, September 22, 2020.
4. Interview of Chandler Davis by author, March 29, 2014.
5. Email from Chandler Davis, September 20, 2020.
6. Further information on the trial and its principals is available in "Of Congressional Witch-Hunts in Academia: The Case of *United States v Horace Chandler Davis*," *Journal of the Historical Society of the United States District Court for the Western District of Michigan* 4 (Summer 2006): 1–22.
7. This paragraph draws on a number of documents from October 1954 in the Chandler Davis FBI files.
8. Theoharis, *Spying on Americans*, 48.
9. James's perspective is available in Schrecker, *No Ivory Tower*, 260–61. His statements to the FBI are contained in memoranda in the Chandler Davis FBI files, January 25, 1954, and July 15, 1954.
10. Memorandum from SAC, Boston, to Director, FBI, in Chandler Davis FBI files, November 19, 1954.
11. Memorandum from SAC, Detroit, to Director, FBI, in Chandler Davis FBI files, November 26, 1954.
12. Transcript of Arguments on Motion to Dismiss Indictment, Box 10, W. Wallace Kent Papers, Bentley Historical Library, University of Michigan.

13. Ibid., 82.
14. Ruling, September 14, 1956, Box 10, W. Wallace Kent Papers, Bentley Historical Library.
15. Email from Chandler Davis, December 12, 2020.
16. Transcript of Proceedings, November 19 and 20, 1956, Box 10, W. Wallace Kent Papers, Bentley Historical Library.
17. Email from Chandler Davis, January 4, 2017.
18. Opinion, June 25, 1957, Box 10, W. Wallace Kent Papers, Bentley Historical Library.
19. Mears, "Of Congressional Witch-Hunts in Academia," 12.
20. On Rauh see Parish, *Citizen Rauh*.
21. *Washington Post*, March 15, 1956.
22. 233 F.2d 681 (DC Cir. 1956).
23. Schwartz, *Super Chief*.
24. Ibid., 236.
25. On Frankfurter, information is drawn from Melvin Urofsky, *Felix Frankfurter Judicial Restraint and Individual Liberties* (Boston: Twayne Publishers, 1991); Feldman, *Scorpions*; Schwartz, *Super Chief*. See also the recent biography by Brad Snyder, *Democratic Justice* (New York: W. W. Norton, 2022).
26. Feldman, *Scorpions*, 9.
27. Urofsky, *Felix Frankfurter*, 5.
28. Ibid., x.
29. Ibid.
30. Ibid., 46.
31. Ibid., 56.
32. Feldman, *Scorpions*.
33. Urofsky, *Felix Frankfurter*, 178.
34. Schwartz, *Super Chief*, 179, quoting from a note from Frankfurter to Harlan in the Felix Frankfurter Papers, Library of Congress.
35. Warren's biography and judicial philosophy are based on White, *Earl Warren*, by Warren's former clerk, G. Edward White.
36. White, *Earl Warren*, 11-12.
37. Ibid., 223.
38. Feldman, *Scorpions*.
39. White, *Earl Warren*, 178-79.
40. Oral arguments for *Watkins*, and other Supreme Court cases, are available at www.oyez.org.
41. Burton's notes on the *Watkins* conference are discussed in Schwartz, *Super Chief*, 235. Douglas's notes are published in Del Dixon, *The Supreme Court in Conference (1940-1985)* (Oxford: Oxford University Press, 2001).
42. Box 29, John Harlan Papers, Special Collections, Princeton University Library.

43. Box 580, Earl Warren Papers, Manuscript Division, Library of Congress.

44. Memo from Douglas to Warren, May 23, 1957, Box 580, Earl Warren Papers, Manuscript Division, Library of Congress.

45. Frankfurter to Chief, May 27, 1957, Box 580, Earl Warren Papers, Manuscript Division, Library of Congress.

46. Warren draft of May 21, 1957 with edits by Frankfurter, Box 580, Earl Warren Papers, Manuscript Division, Library of Congress.

47. Warren draft of May 29, 1957, Box 580, Earl Warren Papers, Manuscript Division, , Library of Congress.

48. Frankfurter edits to second draft and June 5 draft, Box 580, Earl Warren Papers, Manuscript Division, Library of Congress.

49. Frankfurter to Chief, May 31, 1957, Box 580, Earl Warren Papers, Manuscript Division, Library of Congress.

50. Memo from Harlan to Warren, May 31, 1957, Box 29, John Harlan Papers, Special Collections, Princeton University Library.

51. Warren edits to second draft, Box 580, Earl Warren Papers, Manuscript Division, Library of Congress.

52. Memo from Harlan to Chief, June 6, 1957, Box 580, Earl Warren Papers, Manuscript Division, Library of Congress.

53. Frankfurter to Chief, June 5, 1957, Box 580, Earl Warren Papers, Manuscript Division, Library of Congress.

54. 354 US 178.

55. It is unclear whether the double mention of Douglas was an error in place of Brennan or a simple mistake.

56. Frankfurter to Hand, June 30, 1957, Box 105D, Learned Hand Papers, Historical and Special Collections, Harvard Law School Library, quoted with the courtesy and permission of the Harvard Law School.

57. For details see White, *Earl Warren*, 183–84.

58. In 354 US 298 (1957), Harlan wrote that conviction under the Smith Act required establishment of "the advocacy and teaching of concrete action for the forcible overthrow of the Government, and not of principles divorced from action."

59. Further details on the three cases are available in Sabin, *In Calmer Times*.

60. Examples of the press coverage are provided in Sabin, *In Calmer Times*; and Beck, *Contempt of Congress*.

61. *New York Times*, June 18, 1957.

62. *New York Herald Tribune*, June 19, 1957.

63. *I. F. Stone's Weekly*, June 24, 1957.

64. Opinion, June 25, 1957, Box 10, W. Wallace Kent Papers, Bentley Historical Library, University of Michigan.

65. In 244 F.2d 349 (DC Cir. 1957). The same panel had previously affirmed Singer's conviction on a 2–1 vote with Edgerton in the minority.

66. See 247 F.2d 535 (DC Cir. 1957); Beck, *Contempt of Congress*, 115–16; and Schrecker, *No Ivory Tower*, 215–17.

NOTES TO PAGES 168–179   213

67.   Ed Yellin and Jean Fagan Yellin, *In Contempt* (Accord, NY: Alte Books, 2020).
68.   It would be five years and two Supreme Court hearings until his conviction
was reversed by a 5–4 decision over a technicality.
69.   Belknap, *Cold War Political Justice.*
70.   Irons, *The Courage of Their Convictions*, 102.
71.   252 F.2d 129 (DC Cir. 1958).
72.   The two justices were E. Barrett Prettyman and Wilbur Miller.
73.   Email from Chandler Davis, July 11, 2021.
74.   For background on the Institute for Advanced Study, see Steve Batterson,
Pursuit of Genius (Wellesley, MA: A. K. Peters, 2006).
75.   *New York Times*, September 15, 1957.
76.   Biographical information on Harlan and Black is drawn from Tinsley
Yarbrough, *John Marshall Harlan* (New York: Oxford University Press,
1992); and Roger Newman, *Hugo Black* (New York: Pantheon Books,
77.   Yarbrough, *John Marshall Harlan*, 149.
79.   For more on Black and the Ku Klux Klan see Newman, *Hugo Black.*
80.   Feldman, *Scorpions*, 144–47.
81.   An analysis contrasting the applications by Black and Scalia of originalism
to constitutional interpretation is available in Michael Gerhardt, "A Tale
of Two Textualists: A Critical Comparison of Justices Black and Scalia,"
Boston University Law Review 74 (1994): 25–66.
82.   *Carlson v Landon*, 342 US 524 (1952).
83.   On Black's high regard for Meiklejohn see Newman, *Hugo Black.*
84.   On Whittaker's qualifications see Schwartz, *Super Chief*, 215–17.
85.   Dwight Eisenhower, *The White House: Years Mandate for Change, 1953–
1956* (Garden City, NY: Doubleday, 1963), 230.
86.   The first was Samuel Blatchford.
87.   Schwartz, *Super Chief*, 216. For a defense of Whittaker see Smith, *Failing
88.   Schwartz, *Super Chief*, 320.
89.   Irons, *The Courage of Their Convictions*, 102.
90.   Audio of the oral argument is available at www.oyez.org.
91.   Notes on the November 21, 1958, conference are available in Schwartz,
Super Chief, 326; and in Box 1201, William Douglas Papers, Manuscript
Division, Library of Congress.
92.   Box 61, John Harlan Papers, Special Collections, Princeton University
94.   All dated February 11, 1958, in Box 61, John Harlan Papers, Special
Collections, Princeton University Library.
95.   February 13, 1959, draft in Box I–19, William Brennan Papers, Manuscript
Division, Library of Congress.

96. Black's May 28, 1959, draft of what would become his opinion in *Barenblatt* is in Box 337, Hugo Black Papers, Manuscript Division, Library of Congress.

97. Frankfurter to Harlan, June 3, 1959, Box 61, John Harlan Papers, Special Collections, Princeton University Library.

98. Harlan to Frankfurter, June 4, 1959, Box 61, John Harlan Papers, Special Collections, Princeton University Library.

99. 360 US 109 (1959).

100. 269 F.2d 357 (6th Cir. 1959).

101. Petition to the Supreme Court for certiorari by Horace Chandler Davis, filed October 7, 1959, courtesy of Chandler Davis.

102. Email from Chandler Davis, August 2, 2021.

103. Email from Chandler Davis, August 1, 2021.

104. Reply to Government's brief by Frank Donner, filed November 15, 1959, courtesy of Chandler Davis.

105. Bench memorandum on No. 456 by MHB, Box 198, Earl Warren Papers, Manuscript Division, Library of Congress.

106. Mears, "Of Congressional Witch-Hunts in Academia," 13.

107. An article by Chandler about his time in prison is available in Chandler Davis, "So You're Going to Prison," *The Nation* 191 (December 3, 1960): 435–37.

108. 280 F.2d 689 (DC Cir. 1960).

109. 365 US 431 (1961); Bosmajian, *The Freedom Not to Speak*, 152–55.

110. 369 US 749 (1962).

111. 303 F.2d 478 (1962).

9. Fast Forward

1. Natalie discussed surmounting the obstacles in her Academic Freedom Lecture, "Experiencing Exclusion: Scholarship After Inquisition," on October 8, 2015, at the University of Michigan.

2. Interview of Natalie Zemon Davis by author, July 27, 2017.

3. Ibid.

4. Email from Chandler Davis, September 5, 2021.

5. Email from Chandler Davis, August 31, 2021.

6. Interview of Chandler Davis by author, March 29, 2014.

7. Discussions of his results in these areas and their applications are in John Holbrook, "The Mathematics of Chandler Davis," *Mathematical Intelligencer* 36/1 (2014): 6–12; Man-Duen Choi and Peter Rosenthal, "A Survey of Chandler Davis," *Linear Algebra and Its Applications* 208/209 (1994): 3–18.

8. In Gray, "A Committed Life," Chandler discussed several of these activities.

9. Batterson, *Stephen Smale*, 140.

10. The talk was featured at a symposium commemorating the fiftieth anniversary of the Graduate School building. Further details on the events in this paragraph and the next are available in the Introduction of Hollingsworth, *Unfettered Expression*.

11. Email from Chandler Davis, December 11, 2021.
12. Email from Chandler Davis, September 20, 2021.
13. Daniel Golden, "It's Making Us More Ignorant," *The Atlantic*, January 3, 2023.
14. Of the twelve positions six were Trump appointees and one was vacant.

Index

222

INDEX